Jewish Minters & Medalists

Jewish Minters & Medalists

by Daniel M. Friedenberg

Curator of Coins and Medals
The Jewish Museum, New York

Fellow of the
American Numismatic Society

The Jewish Publication Society of America
Philadelphia

First edition

Library of Congress catalog card number: 74-31721
ISBN: 0-8276-0066-6

Printed in the United States of America

FOR

Contents

Acknowledgments

This work would not have been possible without the aid of the following: Dr. Vilem Benda, Director of the State Jewish Museum in Prague; Ms. Marie Chabchay, Director of the Museum of Jewish Art in Paris; Dr. V. Clain-Stefanelli, Curator of Numismatics at the Smithsonian Institution's Museum of History and Technology in Washington, D.C.; Dr. Fülop Ferenc, General Director of the National Museum of Hungary in Budapest; the late Colonel L.S. Forrer; Mr. Friedrich Friedmann, Director of the Money Cabinet of the Historical Museum of Frankfort on Main; Mr. Henry Grunthal, Curator Emeritus of European and Modern Coins at the American Numismatic Society in New York City; Dr. G. Hatz of the Museum of Hamburg History; Ms. Silvia Hurter of the Bank Leu in Zurich; Mr. D. Wayne Johnson, Director of Research for the Medallic Art Company in Danbury, Conn.; the late Dr. Alfred Karger; Mr. Jean Lafaurie of the Medals Cabinet of the National Library in Paris; Mr. Kurt Lombard of Frankfort on Main; Mr. Julius Margolinsky, Librarian of the Jewish Community in Copenhagen; Ms. G. van der Meer of the Royal Coin Cabinet in The Hague; Mr. D. Michael Metcalf of the Ashmolean Museum in Oxford; Dr. V. Potin, Curator of the Coin Cabinet of the Hermitage in Leningrad; Dr. Ira Rezak of New York City; the late Mr. Siegfried Rosenberg; the late Professor Cecil Roth; Dr. Menachem Schmelzer, Librarian of the Jewish Theological Seminary of America in New York City; Dr. Jiří Sejbal, Curator of Coins of the Museum in Brno, Moravia; Mr. Herman Steinberg; Mr. Paul Vincze; the late George Weyr; and Mr. Moshe Zabari of the Toby Pascher Workshop, Jewish Museum in New York City.

Most of all I would like to thank Mr. Arie Kindler, Director of the Kadman Numismatic Museum in Tel Aviv, who generously turned over to me his notes and photographs dealing with Hebrew inscriptions on medieval German coins.

Portions of this book have already been published as two separate articles in *The Numismatist*: "Jewish Minters and Engravers in World Currency" (December 1967) and "Jews and the Art of the Medal" (July 1969).

Photo Credits

American Numismatic Society
British Museum
Historical Museum of Frankfort on Main
Kadman Numismatic Museum
Mr. Kurt Lombard
Mr. Nat Messik
Museum of Hamburg History
Mr. Robert J. Myers
National Museum of Hungary
Royal Coin Cabinet in The Hague
Smithsonian Institution
Mr. Herman Steinberg
Mr. Paul Vincze

Introduction

For a span of almost two millennia, from the crushing of the Bar Kokhba Revolt in 135 C. E. to the establishment of the state of Israel in 1948, there were no coins issued by a Jewish authority. Nevertheless, during this whole period, Jews were actively involved in coinage—as moneyers cutting mint dies, as minters making coins, and as mint masters working either for private profit as lessees or as employees of the state at fixed salaries.

Jewish mint masters in Islamic lands were particularly important in Moslem Spain, Egypt and Turkey. Under certain of the caliphs and emirs of Spain, Jews completely controlled the management of minting and finance. In Egypt, Jews operated the official Fustat mint for the caliphs in a role that was traditionally assigned to them. In the Ottoman Empire, partly as a result of the amazing influence of rich Sephardic emigres from Christian Spain after the expulsion, Jews were important at the Istanbul mint under the early great sultans.

Because the Jews were outside the formal structure of the feudal order in Europe, they had an extraordinarily intimate money relationship to many rulers. Unhindered by the Church's prohibition of all interest, possessing international contacts, proficient by tradition in metal cutting and engraving, and under the exclusive jurisdiction of the king, Jewish tax collectors, business agents, and mint masters had great influence. In the 12th and 13th centuries, when the barter economy was changing to a money economy, there were Jewish mint lessees in almost every European country: in Aragon, Castile, Catalonia, Austria, many German states, Moravia, Hungary, Poland, and possibly England. In the 14th century Jews still controlled mints in various Spanish and German states, as well as Poland. By that time, however, the so-called "pope's usurers" had begun to displace them almost everywhere. A very significant key to the importance of Jews in the economic structure of the earlier medieval period is the appearance of Hebrew or distinctly Jewish names on certain ducal and state currencies, indicating a near monopoly of the nascent money economy.

Though expelled from England in the 13th century, from France in the 14th century, and from Spain in the 15th century, the Jewish presence in mint matters continued in Italy, Germany, and Poland, where the unified national state was slow in evolving. The epoch of European Court absolutism, which paralleled the period of dynastic and religious wars, gave them new opportunities. "Court Jews" and "Coin Jews" made their appearance, especially in the Austrian empire and the other German states. In many ways similar to their predecessors in the medieval period, these Jews used their skills and a web of family and communal contacts to aid their princes, running silver and gold mines, shipping the ore, making and distributing the money.

Jewish emancipation, which received its impetus during the French Revolution and gathered force under Napoleon, led to a new political climate. Although the intimate relationship of Court Jews and Coin Jews to autocratic princes vanished, the Jewish facility in financial matters, born of course out of their exclusion from almost all trades in the feudal order except that of putting money to work at interest, was now freed for use on a higher, national level. The movement from Jewish mint masters to Coin Jews and then to finance ministers represents the spirit of different ages. The number of Jews controlling state mints in the 19th and 20th centuries is truly startling. Despite their small percentage of the general population, and disregarding politics of right or left, the Jews have had an extraordinary representation in state finances since the French Revolution.

The tradition of metal engraving, which led to cutting dies for coinage, drew other Jews to the medallic field. The interdiction in the Jewish religion on making graven images seemed less serious when applied to flat surfaces than those in the round. By the 18th century

Jewish medalists, whose ancestors could also be found among tombstone cutters, seal makers, and pewter and gem engravers, began to come to the forefront. Though particularly evident in the Protestant courts of the Baltic area, Jewish medalists spread in waves east and west, so that by the late 18th century they appeared in Russia, Prussia, the free city of Hamburg, and Belgium.

The first great Jewish medalists worked for despots such as the kings of Prussia and czars of Russia. Their medals exalted the war exploits of their masters, and some of the finest medals of the 18th century depicting Frederick the Great were done by Jacob Abraham and his son Abraham Abramson. Samuel Judin likewise glorified in a series of medals the reign of Peter the Great. The more democratic climate of the 19th century led to new medallic values. Jean-Henri Simon, Belgian by birth, emphasized the cultural contribution of the Low Countries in a series of one hundred medals of illustrious persons. The three Wiener brothers, also Belgian, dominated state engraving (coins, medals, and postage stamps) in their native country for several decades of the late 19th century. A Jewish medalist attained importance early in the history of the United States, and Moritz Furst, who came to America in 1807, was commissioned over and over to do patriotic portraits and commemoratives on the theme of the War of 1812. Wherever cultured wealthy men demanded medallic representation, Jews rose to portray the new bourgeois elite.

The 20th century accelerated this movement. In our country, Victor D. Brenner, a top medalist, in 1909 engraved the head on the Lincoln cent, a design so pleasing it has remained unchanged to this day. In Denmark, Harald Salomon became head of the Danish Royal Mint in 1933, retiring only in 1968. His medals, which uphold the classical principles of clarity and simplicity, are well known. In Germany, Benno Elkan, an excellent sculptor, became a leader in the German revival of plaquettes and medallions; his castings are even surpassed by those of his Austrian peer, Arthur Loewental. The entire medallic art of Hungary from the late 19th century to our time has been dominated by Jews or men born Jews, Fülop O. Beck, Ede Telcs, and Paul Vincze (who has lived in England for many years) being the most noted. Many of the illustrations of the work of these men in this volume show Jewish persons or events, but this is for the convenience of the Jewish collector—actually, these medalists are figures of national importance, and their artistic production stands high in the general cultural history of the last century. In fact, the art of the medal since World War II has gone through a renaissance, and top Jewish sculptors of our time have been increasingly attracted to the field. Among Americans we can include William Zorach, Jacques Lipchitz, Chaim Gross, and Leonard Baskin.

Note must also be made of medalists in the state of Israel. These are Jewish artists living in a Jewish state, with an unqualified allegiance to their old-new land. It is too early to judge whether such persons as Zvi Narkiss, the brothers Shamir, Rothschild and Lippmann, Miriam Karoli, Jean David, Jacob Zim, and Moshe Zipper are on a level with the finest medalists elsewhere. We can state without qualification that many Israeli medals, as can be seen by the illustrations, are of very high caliber. It is questionable whether any other country with such a small and mixed population could produce so uniformly competent and talented a group of designers and engravers.

Jewish mints and minters may have disappeared with the destruction of Judea by the Romans. But the Jewish impact on world coinage and on medal making continued to be tremendous, as is indicated by this study. In our time, almost two thousand years after the Roman conquest, Jews both in the Diaspora and in Israel make extraordinary contributions to the field of coins and medals and the ministry of mints and financial matters related thereto. It is hoped that *Jewish Minters & Medalists* will highlight this contribution.

I Jewish Minters

The development of Zionism among Jews during the latter part of the 19th century led to a marked increase of interest in the coins of the Jewish homeland. Research indicated that these coins fell into distinct groups. The earliest group, and by far the rarest, comprises the Yehud coins, the name given by the Persians to their Judean province. After the revolt of the Maccabees against Greek tyranny, the native Hasmonean rulers issued their own currency. With the coming of the Romans, their puppet Herod and his successors struck currency as well, "of the Jews but not Jewish." Thereafter, during the First Revolt against Rome, the reestablished Jewish authority produced the famous shekels (as well as half and quarter shekels), now the pride of any collector of Jewish antiquities. The last group is the silver and bronze money issued by Bar Kokhba during the Second Revolt, which is of amazingly high aesthetic standards.

Yehud Coin. Judea under Persia
5th and 4th centuries B.C.E.
(double size)

First Jewish Revolt against Rome

Silver Shekel, Year 2

Silver Half Shekel, Year 2

Second Revolt or Bar Kokhba Revolt against Rome

Silver Tetradachm, Year 2. "Shimon"

Silver Denarius, Year 3. "Shimon"

Jewish Kingdoms after the Second Revolt

Although we have no concrete evidence of coins issued by a Jewish authority during the vast stretch of time between 135 and 1948 of the Common Era, that is, between the suppression of the Bar Kokhba Revolt and the revival of the state of Israel, there were in fact four Jewish kingdoms or principalities that existed after the destruction of Judea. They are Khazaria, the Falasha center in northern Ethiopia, Himyara in Yemen, and Mahoza in Babylonia; and the mystery of their currency has yet to be solved.

The Khazars, a Turkish people, settled in the 7th century between the Black and Caspian seas. Sometime before 800 the king and nobility converted to Judaism, followed in the next century by a considerable part of the general populace. The Jewish Khazar kingdom lasted several hundred years. Toward the 10th century it was in decline, the main provinces having been seized by the Russians. Only the Crimea remained to the Khazars, and this territory was conquered at the beginning

British Mandate Money in Palestine
10 Mils, 1927

First Coin of Modern Israel
25 Mils, 1948

of the 11th century. But it can be said without doubt that for over 200 years an independent Jewish kingdom flourished in what is now southern Russia.

Obviously, the money produced in Khazaria would be coinage of a Jewish nation. Yet almost nothing is known of it, and the currency of this Judaized people remains a numismatic mystery. The Khazars were said to control silver mines in the Caucasus from which their troops were paid.[1] They also engaged in extensive trade: Benjamin of Tudela, the famed Jewish traveler, met merchants of Khazaria in Constantinople and Alexandria as late as the 12th century.[2] Such activity could not have been supported by primitive barter alone.

The question of Khazar money is still inconclusive. Eduard von Zambaur, a well-known German numismatist, claims they struck imitations of Arab coinage and that many such coins found in Sweden and Russia originated in Khazar mints.[3] This theory has been attacked by other numismatists. We do know that there is no native Khazar money in the sense of coins bearing the imprint of national kings or symbols; but even establishing the authenticity of the Arab imitations would add an interesting chapter to the history of Jewish coinage.

The case of the Falashas is wrapped in even deeper mystery. This isolated group of black Jews, whose descendants still exist, once formed a powerful kingdom. At its height the Falasha territory included perhaps one-third of modern Ethiopia.[4] As a politically independent people, the Falashas had a distinct historic existence for some thousand years (with intermittent periods of subjugation), terminated only in the 17th century when their heroic chief Gedeon was killed.

It would be expected that within this vast stretch of time the Falashas should have struck money in some form or another – for example, coins in the nearby sacred city and important Christian center of Aksum were issued up to the 8th century with inscriptions in Greek as well as the native tongue of Gheez.[5] (Some rare Aksumitic coins are stamped "Israel" and "Negus

Israel" in Greek, but these refer to a 6th-century Christian king of Aksum with the name "Israel.") For lack of information, therefore, we must assume that the Falasha culture was too primitive to need coinage in those early centuries. Our unique source of information is the royal chronicles of the kings of Ethiopia, and they tell only of battles and war, not of commerce and coinage.

Preceding the Falasha kingdom, but related in history, was Himyara, the ephemeral Jewish monarchy in western Yemen.[6] Jews had settled in the extreme south of Arabia from earliest times, their community being enlarged by refugees from the Roman conquest of Judea. Some five hundred years later, by a combination of natural growth and proselytism, a mixed heathen and Jewish tribe became so powerful it set up its own Jewish state, headed by a monarch, in Yemen. The first of these kings was Abu-Kariba, who converted to Judaism around 500 C.E. His youngest son, Zorah, nicknamed Dhu-Nowas ("curly-locks") for his fine head of hair, followed his father into Judaism and took the Hebrew name of Joseph. Indeed, it was his religious zealousness that brought the young kingdom to ruin, for the Byzantine emperor Justinian, offended by the success of Jewish action against neighboring Christian tribes, encouraged the Christian king Caleb of Aksum in Ethiopia to invade and conquer southern Arabia. Dhu-Nowas committed suicide in 530 rather than yield to the victorious foe. Thousands of Jews were massacred, and the short-lived Jewish kingdom of Himyara disappeared. The survivors and their descendants lived on in the shadows almost another millennium and a half. Their history was completed in the famous "Operation Magic Carpet" air flight when they were brought to Israel in 1949–1950. There is no record of any currency issued from this Jewish kingdom of Yemen.

Another, and even more brief, independent Jewish principality was Mahoza (also spelled Machuza), a Babylonian city on the Tigris River. In the 3rd to 5th centuries this city, inhabited almost entirely by Jews, was overrun again and again as a frontier zone in the wars between the Romans and Persians, creating a spirit of semiautonomy among the citizens. This feeling reached its peak when a reformist movement in the Zoroastrian religion in the early 6th century included among its doctrines the community use of women. King Kobad embraced the doctrine and issued a decree commanding all inhabitants of the Persian Empire to follow suit.

The Jews of Mahoza rose in rebellion against this proclamation, which struck at the roots of their religion. Mar Zutra II, son of the Exilarch (the recognized ruler of the Jewish communities in Babylonia), led the revolt and not only expelled the followers of Zoroaster but also defeated royal troops sent to quell the insurrection. For nearly seven years – from 513 to 520 C.E. – a small independent Jewish kingdom was set up with Mahoza as its capital. Then the Jewish army was overwhelmed by the Persian troops, Mar Zutra executed with his aged grandfather, and the inhabitants of the city stripped of their possessions and dispersed. Once again, there is no indication whatsoever that this short-lived Jewish principality issued any coinage.

Aside from these exotic kingdoms, there is one odd "Jewish state" that did produce money. This involves the strange case of Julius Popper, dating from less than a century ago.[7] The history of Popper appears in not

Julius Popper
Tierra del Fuego, Argentina
One Gram

Five Grams

one of the standard textbooks of Argentine history, and yet it represents a vivid, though admittedly minor, episode in that country's development. Popper, a Romanian Jewish adventurer, arrived in Argentina during the 1880s. He moved to the extreme south, to the sparsely settled land of Tierra del Fuego, where he created a vast feudal-type estate.

In 1889 Popper issued two varieties of gold coins (as well as stamps), weighing one and five grams. The one-gram coin is inscribed "El Paramo," which means "a high and cold region" in Spanish. The five-gram coin is inscribed "Lavaderos de Oro del Sur," or "Washers of Gold of the South," referring to washing gold from the river sands, the source of Popper's wealth. These pieces, now in great demand among numismatists, are the only gold coins ever issued by a Jew before the emergence of modern Israel. Incidentally (though there are conflicting reports), Popper was arrested by the Argentine authorities and committed suicide at Buenos Aires in 1893.

Though no Jewish state coins can properly be said to have been struck between the Bar Kokhba Revolt and the revival of the state of Israel, there is another category of currency of Jewish interest. This is coinage made or issued by Jewish moneyers or mint masters either as employees of the state or as private lessees. In general, as employed here, a minter is a person involved in the making of money, a mint master a person running a mint for private profit, and a moneyer a person involved in the cutting of mint dies.

Jewish Minters in Moslem Lands

Jewish minters were active in Moslem countries from the beginning. Although the records are not crystal clear, it appears that Sumeir (meaning a dark-complected person in Arabic) made mint dies and was in charge of striking coins for Caliph Abdul Melek (685–705) of Damascus. Since the first Moslem coins were struck at this time, this would make Sumeir one of the technical founders of Islamic coinage.[8]

Jews also held mint positions in Egypt from earliest time. According to Graetz,[9] Jewish goldsmiths in pre-Moslem days at Alexandria were already involved in mint affairs. After the Arab invasion, they continued this role, especially at the Fustat mint operated by the caliphs. Even after the Turks took over, minting was traditionally assigned to Jews, who received the official title of Saraf-Baschi, or Head Minter, from the Turks, which also included supervision over the Customs House.

Sumeir
Falu of Caliph Abdul Melek. 7th Century

We are indebted to Professor S. Goitein[10] for considerable insight into the workings of this system at Fustat in the 11th through the 13th centuries. The low status of Jews in Egypt at this time reinforced their traditional role as metal engravers and goldsmiths. Caliphs preferred employing Jews since it was easier to punish them for irregularities or confiscate their wealth than it would have been with influential Moslems. Furthermore, working with hot metals in the heat of Egypt was unpleasant, and Moslems avoided the trade.

The records of the Cairo Geniza (a storehouse of Hebrew documents thoroughly analyzed only in recent years) reveal something of the mint system and even of some of the men who figured prominently in it. The Jews did not work for salaries but created partnerships, taking each job for the profit it yielded. The partnerships included specialized functions, with a director, an administrator, and an agent. Apparently, technical talent was pooled with money to capitalize the operation, and the profits split accordingly. We know that Japheth ben Abraham, in partnership with two other

Jews, was administrator of the Fustat mint around 1086. Another brief mention is made of two Jewish partners working the caliphal mint in the latter part of the 12th century. And in 1219 a former mint official wrote a letter in which he mentioned two other Jews working in the mint at that time; one named Kazaruni, a name of Persian origin. It is obvious from these casual references that there must have been many other Jews at the Fustat mint during the medieval period, since the documents refer only to correspondence or rabbinic court actions due to difficulties.

Until recently, Isaac Hacohen Shalal (more properly Sholal in direct translation from the Hebrew sources) was known solely as Nagid or head of the Jewish community in Cairo before the Turkish conquest. Rich and held in high esteem by the Mameluke sultan, he was dismissed in 1517. Thanks to a letter[11] discovered in the Cairo Geniza, certain new information clarifies events. This letter informs us that Shalal owed his princely power to his high position in the Egyptian treasury, where he served as director of the mint from 1502 to 1517. After the Turkish conquest, Shalal retired to Jerusalem and died there in 1524. Since Isaac Hacohen Shalal had inherited the office as Nagid of the Jewish community in Cairo from his relative Nathan Hacohen Shalal – a perquisite that depended on money and political influence – this lends further evidence to Graetz's statement that the Jews traditionally ran the Egyptian mint.

When Sultan Selim I conquered Egypt in 1517 he appointed Abraham de Castro, a Jew of Spanish descent, to be master of the mint and coin the new Turkish money. Abraham de Castro has another claim to fame. Several years later, the Egyptian viceroy, Ahmad Shaitan, tried to separate the country from Turkish rule and set himself up as an independent king. When Abraham de Castro was ordered to strike the new Egyptian coinage, he secretly left Egypt and reported the matter to Istanbul. Ahmad was so enraged that he made plans to kill all the Jews. This was barely averted by his overthrow through a palace revolution in 1524, an event that the Egyptian Jews celebrated for many years with a local Purim. Abraham de Castro was reinstated as mint master, and, though the records are not clear, there is some indication that his family received the grant of the mint for many years thereafter.[12]

We also know that more than a century later, in the 1660s, the Cairo mint master was Raphael Joseph Chelebi (Halabi), originally from Aleppo. Chelebi was a rather odd combination of enormous wealth combined with deep mystic yearnings. He supported some fifty talmudists and cabbalists, wore the garments of a penitent, and often ordered himself flaggelated. As might be expected, Chelebi fell prey to the delusions of the pseudo-Messiah Sabbetai Zevi.[13]

The Ottoman Empire in those centuries had expanded deep into Europe. As in Cairo, Jews also were involved with mint matters at the capital city of Istanbul. Under Murad III (1574–1595), the director of the Turkish mint was a Jew, Hodja Nessimi (or Nissim).[14] In this same period, Moses Benveniste – known to the Turks as Hodja Moussahibi – was involved in the debasement of the Turkish currency, which inspired a revolt of the janissaries in 1589.[15]

Jews and the Money Structure of Medieval Europe

Jews played a very important role in the money structure of medieval Europe, especially during the 11th to 13th centuries, when the economy was transformed from a barter to a money system. The Church's prohibition of interest (usury being defined as any interest, not just high interest) and the multi-ethnic nature of such areas as the Iberian peninsula and the Holy Roman Empire gave them exceptional opportunities, which were magnified by the fact that Jews were outside the formal structure of feudal society.

As a result, early trade routes dominated by Jewish merchants were soon established from Germany to Bohemia and to Italy, as well as farther east. Another line of trade ran through the Mediterranean, from

Spain to Egypt. These Jewish merchants formed a homogeneous group, for both mutual advantage and protection, and were the obvious link in the primitive international monetary system.

On the national level, the special talents of the Jews made them particularly suited to handle mint matters. Metal cutting and engraving were old Jewish professions, and the Jewish goldsmith was a universal type — it was a short step from being a goldsmith to cutting dies. Furthermore, the widespread nature of Jewish contacts became a valuable asset in the evolving economy. To administer financial affairs, it was necessary to know the international money market, to have connections, and to buy metals and circulate coins.

Another important element that brought Jews close to mintage was their special relation to royalty. The king alone had exclusive jurisdiction over the Jews — not the clergy, or the nobles, or the towns. They belonged to the Crown, to the royal patrimony. Alfonso III of Aragon-Catalonia explicitly stated, "All Jews are under the protection and safeguard of the king. . . . The Jews are the king's men; their punishment is detrimental to the king." The bad aspect of this position was that the reverse also held, that is, it was equally the prerogative of a king, due to religious fanaticism or other factors, to expel the Jews without their having any opportunity to appeal. This, of course, happened at one time or another in almost every country. But in the early medieval period, before the Italians and Germans began money lending, it was against the self-interest of the king to do this. Surrounded by court intrigue and uncertain of the ambitions of his nobles, the kings leaned heavily on their Jewish tax collectors, mint masters, and business agents because their fidelity was not threatened by conflicting loyalties. It may also be mentioned that in this period a minimum of ten percent of a king's income was derived through Jewish money lending, and it was most often the surest form of revenue. This also created a personal intimacy based on the field of money.

Jewish Minters in Western Europe

A considerable number of European coins stamped with Hebrew inscriptions or with the names or initials in Hebrew or Latin of Jewish mint masters or moneyers still survive today.[16]

French records indicate the earliest recorded example of a Jewish moneyer in all Europe. It is almost a certainty that one of the minters for King Clotaire of Burgundy, who issued the royal coins at Chalon-sur-Saône around 555 C.E., was a Jew. The case has been explored fully by the Vicomte d'Amecourt, specialist on Merovingian money, and decided in the affirmative.[17] "The Jew Priscus," who coined some of the most attractive money of this period with his partner Domnolus, was also a favorite goldsmith and designer of jewelry for King Chilperic, who succeeded Clotaire.

The sole argument against this hypothesis is the existence of another Priscus in the same period, a bishop of nearby Lyons. Bishops were often moneyers at this time, and it also appears that Domnolus, the fellow minter with Priscus, became a bishop later in life.

After weighing all the evidence pro and con, Vicomte d'Amecourt concludes "these texts seem to indicate quite clearly" that the moneyer was the Jew Priscus. He adds that there was nothing contradictory in a Jew's being a minter in this period, since moneyers were often goldsmiths, a favorite Jewish profession. In fact, d'Amecourt points out that at Mâcon, near Chalon, and precisely in the time of Priscus, there was a moneyer named Juse (or Jusef), a name strange to all but Jews in the Gallo-Roman area. For the same reason of nomenclature, d'Amecourt feels that other minters named Jaco (or Jacote) and Osias, operating in this century, were also Jews.[18]

However, much later in France, the case of Louis de Saporta is well documented. A Marrano apparently considered a Christian, he was minter at Toulouse in 1588, 1589, and for three months of 1590, that is, at the time of the assassination of Henry III and the coming to power of Henry IV, when France was riven by

French Jewish Moneyers

Priscus
Moneyer at Chalon-sur-Saône
Gold Tremissis, c. 555 C.E. (enlarged five times)
PRISCVS DOMNOLUS

Jacote
Moneyer at Orleans
Gold Tremissis, 6th Century (triple size)
IACOTE MO

Juse (or Jusef)
Moneyer at Mâcon
Gold Tremissis, 6th Century (triple size)
IVSE MONETARIVS

religious conflict. His mark, still in evidence on coins, was "S." Louis de Saporta took orders from Paris, and his dismissal in 1590 by the rebellious Catholic provincial leaders is an interesting aspect of the conflict between the monarchs and the Ultramontane party.[19]

In exactly this same period appeared Simon de Navarre, also a Marrano, who likewise worked under Henry IV at Compiègne (a city to the north of Paris) from 1591 to 1595, and perhaps at nearby Melun as well. On the coins of Simon de Navarre appear the small mark in Hebrew of the letter "shin," undoubtedly standing for the first letter of his name: that is, "Shimon," the Hebrew original of the name Simon. There is some indication the currency was unauthorized, but since the issue was redeemed at par value for legal coinage, the circumstances must have related to Henry IV's subsequent victory in the civil war then raging.[20]

Jewish moneyers were evident in Catalonia by the early 11th century.[21] References are made throughout the reign of Count Berenguer Ramon I of Barcelona

Louis de Saporta
Moneyer of Toulouse under Henry III and Henry IV, 1588–1590
Mark: S
Gold Ecu, 1588
(Left: HENRICVS III. D.G. FRAN. ET. POL. REX S 1588)

Simon de Navarre
Moneyer for Henry IV at Compiègne, 1591–1595
Mark: W. (Hebrew letter for "S" standing for "Simon")
Quarter Ecu, 1591
(Left: SIT NOMEN DOMINI BENEDICTVM W)

Spanish Jewish Moneyer

Bonnom
Moneyer of Catalonia under Count Berenguer Ramon I
11th Century
(Right: Note name in Latin letters on last line.)

(1018–1035) to Bonnom the Hebrew – that is, Shem Tov – and in 1023 a debt is mentioned of money in gold "struck by Bono Nomen the Hebrew goldsmith." Although Bonnom cut his coin inscriptions in the conventional Arabic used in most of Spain at the time, he had the curious custom of inscribing his name in Latin letters. His coins were still reported to be circulating almost half a century after his death, and several examples are still extant.[22]

In 1066 Count Ramon I Berenguer (1035–1076), son of the aforementioned, sold the right to mint silver coinage for five years to two Christian minters and to David bar Jacob the Hebrew.[23] Again in Barcelona, Benveniste de Porta, who was also bailiff of the city (his brother was the famous Rabbi Nahmanides), leased the mint under James I of Aragon-Catalonia (1213–1276).[24] A century later, in 1372, under Pedro IV (1336–1387), Vidal de la Cavalleria leased the gold currency of Aragon-Catalonia in partnership with a Christian citizen of Saragossa, the king's treasurer.[25] In this same period, the royal mint was leased to a totally Jewish company.[26] In the last case, although our information is not exact (and there may even be an overlap between the two companies mentioned), Pedro IV threatened to expel the entire Jewish community at one point because of alleged misdeeds on the part of his Jewish mint masters.[27]

The Jews in Castile had deep roots in the mint. In 1287 and 1288 Sancho IV actually surrendered to Abraham el Barchilon (the Barcelonian) practically all the revenues of the kingdom, including the concession to mint the royal coinage.[28] And Alfonso XI (1312–1350) leased the mint to Don Samuel Aben Huacar (Ibn Wakar), who deliberately debased the currency and thus caused violent feelings against the Jews. This in turn led to Don Samuel's death by torture, although he was both physician and astrologer to the king.[29]

Whether Jews were minters in England is still undecided.[29a] There is no evidence of Jews residing there in any organized group before William the Conqueror in 1066; and in 1290 they were expelled. Between the expulsion and their reacceptance in 1655, the occasional Marranos had no relation to the mint. We must therefore look to the 12th and 13th centuries for information.

The special relation of the Jews to the king during the apogee of feudalism has already been remarked upon. This relationship was especially strong in England, and it is known that William the Conqueror invited a group of Jews from Rouen to England to get the feudal dues paid to the royal treasury in coin rather than in kind, a task that required a special body of king's men separate from the population. Because of the Church edict against interest, the Jews rose rapidly in fortune. It was not until the coming of the Italian merchants, the so-called "pope's usurers," that the Jews became less valuable to the king; and they were ultimately expelled at the end of the 13th century. But in earlier years, especially during the reign of Henry II (1154–1189), their position was of great importance in treasury matters. In fact, the value of the personal property of the Jews under Henry II was regarded as one-fourth of that of the whole country, and Aaron of Lincoln was the wealthiest person in all England.

The Jews were often treasury agents, making advances at interest to the Crown on the security of the local taxation, and this close relation brought them into the realm of mint matters. There is some evidence that Jews may have been minters.

A find of 6,000 silver pennies at Eccles from this period is an important source of information. Among the names of the minters, which were invariably listed on the reverses, are several of Old Testament origin.[30] These include Isac of Everwic (York), Samuel of Can (Canterbury), and Salemun, also of Canterbury. In favor of the thesis, we know there were significant communities of Jews at both York and Canterbury. Furthermore, the records indicate an Isac son of Moses and an Isac Blund, both of York, in this period, as well as a Samuel son of Jacob at Canterbury. Based on these relations, Hubert Hall, in his *Court Life Under the Plantagenets,* regards Isac as a Jewish minter. Against the thesis, none of these men is mentioned as "monetarii," a description required at the time. Equally significant in the negative sense is the fact that minters had to take an oath of fealty based on a Christian formula that a Jew could not accept.

A more comprehensive study of British coin hoards indicates some of the same Old Testament names and others as well.[31] Samuel of Canterbury appears in three separate hoards from the reigns of Henry II, John, and Henry III. Salemu, or Salemun, of Canterbury reappears. An Abel of London also appears in three separate hoards under these monarchs. A Jacob of Bristol and a Jacob of Norwich appear, respectively, in two and three separate hoards during the rule of Henry III. Under Henry II there appears in one hoard a Daniel of Salisbury and in another hoard a Sawul (Saul) of Gloucester.

The evidence is too spotty to allow definite conclusions. There is no record of a Jewish community in this period at Salisbury, which would seem to eliminate Daniel. Also, it is to be noted that a deposit of almost one thousand coins uncovered at Chester from around 970 – that is, previous to the entry of the Jews into England – also included a minter with the name Daniel. It was not uncommon for Christians to have surnames based on the Old Testament, though names such as Salomon and Saul would probably have been rare. Perhaps the sole affirmative factual evidence, though it is hardly conclusive, is the record under Henry II according to which three Jews forfeited a sum of money to be quit of a charge of "cambivisse." The word refers to exchanging, which, however was not a crime; it may also be construed as minting, which was.[32] After reviewing the evidence, the leading writer on the subject, Joseph Jacobs, feels that the Old Testament names alone are not sufficient to prove the existence of Jewish minters in this period of English history. This opinion is supported by the late Cecil Roth, the foremost authority on English Jewry. Though he too, wrote of

Purported Jewish Minters in England
12th and 13th Centuries

Abel of London
Silver Penny
HENRICVS (Henry)
ABEL . ON . LUNDE

Samuel of Canterbury
Silver Penny
HENRICVS
SAMUEL . ON . CAN.

Salemun of Canterbury
Silver Penny
HENRICVS
SALEMUN . ON . C

Jacob of Norwich
Silver Penny
HENRICVS REX III
IACOB . ON . NORWI

Isac of York and also mentioned a David of Thetford,[33] in conversation with the writer Dr. Roth expressed the opinion that these men were possibly not Jews.

There is one certain example in medieval Italy of a Jewish mint master. Around the year 1000 Samuel Amittai, of a distinguished Italian Jewish family, administered the mint at Capua, a small city north of Naples.[34] Karl Schwarz, in the short article "Muenzjude," written for the *Juedisches Lexikon* (Berlin, 1930), also states that in the 10th century a Jewish mint master by the name of Gideon operated in Milan, but the author has been unable to track down the information to a primary source.

Later, however, the little duchy of Correggio, attached to Modena in northern Italy, was the scene of some colorful events under Prince Siro, who began his reign in 1605 and was deposed in 1630. Siro, involved in a series of activities among which the debasement of money was merely one vice, farmed the mint in his early years to two Jewish mint masters, Abraham Jaghel and David Ricco.[35] Abraham Jaghel was himself a Renaissance type, for aside from his dubious situation as a mint master to Siro, he was also a noted writer and philosopher.

The dukes of Modena likewise began to employ Jewish mint masters in this period, some of whom also were involved in fraudulent money schemes. A series of nine Jews or Jewish companies ran the mint for the Estensi for over 150 years, from Joseph Teseo of Correggio (1630) to the Bosnian, Fortunato Attias (1794).[36]

Jewish Minters in Central and Eastern Europe

As we move east, Jewish participation in these matters is clearly established. Our knowledge actually precedes the Christian epoch, for Jewish purveyors operated with the Roman legions in Western Germany and Central Europe, staying on as traders after the spread of Christianity.

Vienna was an early crossroads of trade. Already by the early 13th century a Responsum issued by the

Viennese Rabbi Isaac ben Moses prohibited a Jewish master of the mint from allowing his Christian employees to stamp money on the Sabbath.[37] In fact, the first record of a Viennese Jew is that of a mint master, Schlom (Solomon), who operated mints for Duke Leopold V of Austria (1177–1194) both in Vienna and in the nearby suburb of Vienna-Neustadt.[38] Schlom, who was also in charge of the ducal finances and customs, became so powerful that he was singled out and killed by Crusaders passing through Vienna in 1196. There is some evidence that Schlom had emigrated from Spain,[39] which illustrates the internationalism involved in this trade.

Indeed, the Austrian Jewish relation to the treasury was so close under the Babenberg dukes that in 1222 a special decree was imposed by the nobility, which stipulated that Counts of the Treasury and officers of the mint had to be noblemen and could not under any circumstances be Jews.[40] The decree was violated almost immediately, for it would seem that a Jew by the name of Techanus (spelled in other documents variously as Teha, Tehanus, and Tekanus) soon followed Schlom as ducal administrator of finances and customs, and possibly as a mint master as well. Although Techanus is first mentioned in Hungary, he apparently moved to Vienna before 1235.[41] We also know that Ottakar II (1254–1278) ignored the decree and hired Jews as masters of the mint.[42] Lublin and his brother Nekelo are specifically mentioned in one document.[43]

Perhaps most surprising is that some feudal lords and high ecclesiastics in the heart of the Holy Roman Empire, as well as in nearby German territories, employed Jewish mint masters and even gave them the right to stamp their coins in Hebrew. Rather large bracteates, thin, one-sided silver coins, were issued between 1170 and 1180 at Wetterau – the old German princely state of Hesse – with the name "David Hacohen" clearly stamped in Hebrew.[44] They probably were produced at Frankfort on Main under Kuno von Minzenburg (1151–1212), considered a protector of the Jews in

David Hacohen
Bracteate, issued under Kuno von Minzenburg at Frankfort on Main, 1170-1180
Enlargement

Actual size

Unknown Jewish Mint Master
Bracteate, issued under Otto the Rich, Margrave of Meissen, 1156–1190

Jechial
Minter for Bishop Otto von Lobdenburg, 1207–1223
Silver Denar

Enlargement of denar reverse showing "Jechial" in Hebrew letters on bottom line

Unknown Jewish Minter from the Abbey of Lorsch
Half Bracteate, issued under Heinrich, 1153–1167

those difficult Crusading days. In nearby Swabia – the location being determined by the style of bracteate – a minter by the name of Shmuel (Samuel) cut his name in Hebrew letters on the ducal bracteates of this period.[45] We know nothing more of Shmuel, though Jews are mentioned in Swabian records in the second half of the 12th century.

At this same time Otto the Rich (1156–1190), Margrave of Meissen – a city near Dresden – must have also employed a Jewish minter, for one of his bracteates shows worn Hebrew letters on the rim.[46] Related to this is a bracteate from the Eisenach-Gotha region, issued between 1208 and 1215 (the dates being established from the rest of the hoard), showing on the outer rim Hebrew letters which, according to a report by Professor M. Lidzbarski, read "Gershom."[47] Another bracteate from Pegau – near Leipzig in Saxony – shows eight smudged Hebrew letters; and at nearby Luzice there is similar evidence of Hebrew letters on coins.[48] Also we know of a "lion" bracteate from Saxony of Duke Bernhard I (1180–1212), with what seem to be Hebrew letters.[49]

A very special example is that of Bishop Otto von Lobdenburg (1207–1223) at the ecclesiastical court of Wuerzburg – in south central Germany – who had a Jewish minter by the name of Jechial for quite a few years.[50] The name "Jechial" is clearly marked on numerous denars, a small silver coin type stamped on both sides. Jews also ran the mint in the ecclesiastical court of Trèves for almost a century, from about 1260 to 1350.[51] They may even have been employed directly by other Jews (or combined as one function the roles of financial adviser and lessee), for from 1341 to 1347 Jacob ben Nathaniel (or Daniel) was treasurer to the archbishop.[52] And at the abbey of Lorsch – just outside Worms – a bracteate from the mid-12th century shows four Hebrew letters inserted in the corners created by the cross on the reverse. These, according to a study by Professor Schall of the University of Heidelberg, spell out in ancient and modern Hebrew letters "To Your

Lordship," apparently referring to the reigning abbot of Lorsch.[53] The writer has some doubt as to this interpretation. It is obvious from the widely separated areas, however, that stamping Hebrew on coins, indicating Jewish minters or lessees, was a common practice in the German states during the 12th and 13th centuries.

The question of early Bohemian Jewish mint masters is still undecided. Certain names, according to leading philologists of Central Europe, would seem to be Jewish. The matter is complicated by the fact that the names were stamped in Latin on the coins, not Hebrew, and thus possibly distorted by transliteration; furthermore, the letters of the names are often in different order or show different spelling on various dies.[54] Working for Bogislaus II at the Prague mint in the latter part of the 10th century, their names stamped on denars, were: Omeriz, whose dies sometimes indicate Omer or Omerz; Nacub or Nacubin; and Mizleta. In this same period at the Visegrad mint worked Zanta or Znata.

Opinions as to whether these men were Jews are not unanimous. Gustav Skalsky thought they possibly were. Viktor Katz, an extremely gifted Czech numismatist and a Jew himself, was also inclined to the affirmative. In our time, the esteemed Czech medievalist Francis X. Cach merely states there is no concrete proof one way or the other.

We also know from the *Chronicle* of the 12th-century Czech Kosmas (Book II, Chapter 21) that an 11th-century converted Jew by the name of Podiva established a fortress in Moravia on the Austrian frontier. Called Podivin after him (now called Kostel), this location was the earliest site of customs clearance and money issue in Moravia; and since Podiva was the lord, it must be presumed that he was the lessee or mint master if the money was struck in his time.

There is, however, no question that the Bohemian king Wladislaus II (1158–1173) had a Jewish minter in Lusatia, that part of present East Germany between the Elbe and Oder rivers: a bracteate with a Hebrew inscription in the center is known.[55]

Omeriz
Working for Bogislaus II at the Prague Mint, 967–999
Silver Denar (read right to left)
OMERIZ PRAGA CIV.
BOELESLAUS DUX

Unknown Jewish Mint Master
Probably under Ottakar II
Bracteate, issued in Moravia, 13th century
(double size)

Furthermore, though the exact background still needs clarification, there is concrete evidence of Hebrew on coins found in southern Moravia. An extraordinary hoard of some 1200 coins was unearthed in 1959 at Střelice, among which, according to report, were over fifty bearing the same Hebrew inscription. From the late 12th or 13th century, they are related iconographically to bracteates of Otto I of Brandenburg (1170–1184). Dr. Jiří Sejbal, Curator of Coins of the Moravian Museum, kindly sent the writer a cast of a typical bracteate. Though some of the Hebrew letters are blurred and others rubbed out, it is possible to translate tentatively "Great Honor to You Ottakar."

This could refer to the Bohemian king Přemysl Ottakar I (1197–1230), who, though not ruler of Moravia, had strong influence there. It could also refer to Přemysl Ottakar II, Margrave of Moravia from 1248 to 1253 and thereafter king. In 1254 this later Ottakar issued a Bill of Rights to the Jews, employed Jewish mint masters in Austria in defiance of a special decree, and was considered a friend of the Jewish communities. Adding evidence that these coins were issued by Ottakar II is the fact that in the period 1197–1253 denars were struck in Moravia, bracteates appearing only after this date, which, of course, coincides with the accession of the later Ottakar. On the other hand, internal evidence seems to indicate the hoard was hidden before this time. Naturally, we cannot exclude the hypothesis that the bracteates were brought into Moravia from Bohemia, at this point only a short distance away; and indeed German bracteates from Saxony were also found in this same area.

As an intriguing detail, the bracteates in question are quite thin, which might mean that the Jewish mint masters deliberately reduced the silver content for reasons similar to those that occurred a bit earlier in Poland, which will be discussed shortly. When the entire Moravian hoard can be analyzed, these coins will add greatly to our knowledge of the web of Jewish mint masters extending throughout most of Europe during the apogee of the medieval period.

The history of Hebrew on coins of Hungary is a fascinating bypath in general European numismatics. The Magyar leaders accepted Christianity in 975, but, in fact, only the court became Christian, the people remaining pagan for the most part (much as the Khazar leaders in the Crimea became Jewish two centuries earlier). There were two pagan risings in the 11th century. Béla IV (1235–1270) brought in Cuman pagan colonists in such vast numbers that they almost overwhelmed the Christian population. Then Béla married his son Stephan (István) – later Stephan V (1270–1272) – to a Cuman woman. The result was that the Holy See launched a Hungarian Crusade to prevent the lapse of the kingdom into paganism, and Stephan's son, Ladislaus IV, perished in the conflict.[56]

Given this background, it can be seen that these early Hungarian rulers during the Arpad period had no objection to Jewish mint masters. A Responsum by Rabbi Judah Hacohen of Mainz (Mayence) informs us that around 1063 Queen Anastasia, widow of Andreas I, had dealings with Hungarian and German Jewish businessmen regarding the use of the royal mint. As a result, one merchant was permitted to have his own small silver coins struck there. This, however, was a private minting.[57]

The connection became more official by the 13th century, when state policy changed and the mint began to be farmed out. Between the years 1222 and 1234 the clergy and nobility protested vehemently against the role of Jewish mint masters, and the matter was not settled until 1239, when Pope Gregory IX decided in favor of the Jewish interests. This tolerance continued until 1279, when the pressures grew more extreme and Jews were excluded.[58]

Though Jewish mint masters operated during the rule of Andreas II (1205–1235) and of Ladislaus IV (1272–1290), it is commonly considered that no Hebrew stampings were used. The writer has some doubt, for in the classic work on Hungarian coinage, *Corpus Nummorum Hungariae*, by Réthy and Probszt,[59] the line drawings for the coins of Andreas II (Plate XIII, items nos. 226 and 227) show a letter that might easily be a Hebrew "tet"; and this letter also appears on the immediate subsequent coinage as well. Without question, however, under Béla IV, and even more during the brief two-year reign of his son Stephan V, Hebrew letters appear on the state currency, on denars and half-sized denars, called obols. The Budapest Jewish Museum exhibits a half dozen examples, and there are others in the collections of the Hungarian National Museum and the Kadman Numismatic Museum in Tel Aviv, Israel.

The identification of both the meaning of these letters

and the actual letters themselves has been somewhat of a mystery. Réthy and Probszt have complicated the matter by spinning the axis of some of these coins in the plates, where they use line drawings rather than the more accurate photographs, thus leading one to imagine the letters are different than they actually are. A common Hebrew letter on the coins of Béla IV is the "tet," the Latin *T*, which has often been thought to be the Hebrew letter "peh," or *P*, because of the aforementioned swinging of the axis of these coins when reproduced. The other common Hebrew letter is the "tsadi," for which there is no exact comparable Latin letter, the sound being closest to the slur of the two end letters in the contraction *that's*. The Hebrew letters appear in the center of the obverse of these coins, sometimes with the king's name inscribed round, other times within a wreath, and less frequently coupled with a three-leafed flower. The reverses are adorned with conventional medieval symbols, like an angel killing a dragon, a tower or castle between lilies, or a face with a flag and the Latin "Agnus Dei" or "Lamb of God."

The most common Hebrew letter used during the short reign of Stephan V is the "aleph," or Latin *A*, about whose identification there is no question. The other Hebrew letter is the "shin," the sound of *sh* in words like *show* or *shop*. The position of this letter between two birds, possibly doves, matches exactly the "aleph" between the same two birds aforementioned on the other coins of Stephan V, so it is almost certain we are dealing with a "shin." The obverses of these coins are always stamped with the head of Stephan facing left, sometimes with his name spelled round and other times with "Hungarian money" spelled in Latin in two variant forms. The line drawings of Réthy and Probszt (Plate XVI, items nos. 292 and 293) seem to indicate another indecipherable Hebrew letter, but the writer feels this is a badly drawn "aleph" as well, particularly since the coin types are identical with those clearly showing "aleph."

Little research has been done on these coins, and we are not quite sure of their background. Probably the letters stood for the marks or initials of Jews who farmed the mint under these rulers. Perhaps at the end of the reign of Andreas II, and then continuing under Béla IV, the mint was farmed to a Jew whose name began with T, or who assumed this identifying mark. A similar function was performed under Béla IV by a Jew with the initial or mark of "Ts." When Stephan V came to the throne, Jews contracting the mint had the initials or marks of "A" and "Sh." It is intriguing to think of these unknown men, dead for over seven hundred years, whose sole stamp in history is a single Hebrew letter.

Of all countries that had Hebrew inscriptions on their coinage, the case of Poland is unique. Again the historical setting is relevant. The year 1966 was officially proclaimed as the 1000th Jubilee of Christianity in Poland. With all due respect, it must be stated that the year 966 was the introduction, not the institution, of Polish Catholicism. For several hundred years the new religion did not crystallize. It was only in the 12th century – 1124 to 1128 – that Pomerania became converted to Christianity and Boleslaus III, in the words of the *Encyclopedia Britannica*, succeeded in "making head against paganism generally."[60] The amazing events to be described occurred within fifty years of that time. They are backed in a detailed study made by Professor Marian Gumowski[61] of some 320 coins with Hebrew inscriptions.

A capsule survey of the extremely complex Polish history must be made in order to understand this coinage. Boleslaus IV (1146–1173) was succeeded by Mieszko III, called Mieszko the Older, to the throne of Great Poland. This corresponded roughly to the area of Western and Central Poland as we know it today, including the lands incorporated from Germany after World War II.

Mieszko III, for reasons to be discussed, was deposed in 1177 and his lands split up. The main body of Poland went to Casimir II, or the Just (1177–1199), the younger brother of Mieszko; while Silesia was given to Boleslaus

Hungarian Money by Unknown Jewish Mint Masters, 13th Century

Obols, issued under Béla IV, 1235–1270

Angel Killing Dragon

"BELAE REX" round; "Tet" in center

Enlargement

Half Moon with Castle between Two Lilies

Wreath; "Tsadi" in center

Obols, issued under Stephan (István) V, 1270–1272

"MONETA UNGARIE" round; king's head in center

Two birds facing one another; "Aleph" in center

Enlargement

"REX STEPNS" round; king's head in center

Two birds facing one another; "Shin" in center

the High (1177–1201), another brother.

In 1181 Mieszko succeeded in retaking part of the territory, with the important Cracow area still in the hands of Casimir the Just. Mieszko's oldest son, Odo (1177–1194), had supported the revolt and retained the province of Posen. Mieszko himself was soon compelled to give up part of the territories he had reconquered. His second son, called Mieszko the Younger (1186-1194), received the province of Kalisch. And his youngest son, Boleslaus (1186–1195), got the territory of Kuiawy (Kujavien). Mieszko retained Gniezno (Gnesen) and, as part of the general redistribution, got back Upper Silesia from Boleslaus the High. Oddly, these rulers predeceased Mieszko without leaving heirs, and it thus happened that at the end of his life the various provinces reverted back to a unified control. Thus Mieszko III had two definite periods of rule, the first from 1173 to 1177 over all of Great Poland, and the second from 1181 to 1202, during which time the area over which he ruled fluctuated in size. It is necessary to understand these changes, for all the rulers issued coins at the same time at the end of the 12th century.

The predecessor to Mieszko, Boleslaus IV, struck traditional solid silver denars. He employed Jews, who were entering Poland during this period in flight from German persecutions. Some of these Jews, as we know from the previous history, were skilled goldsmiths and minters, and they were used in various mint offices. But they were wholly subservient to the king, and no Hebrew appears on their coins.

Mieszko III had other ideas, based on a mixture of avarice and necessity.[62] On one hand he wanted to expand his empire and needed money to buy friends and make war. On the other hand, facing the threat of numerous feudal overlords in that epoch, he was anxious to weaken the power of his surly princes. His solution — which in certain ways resembled that of the kings of the Christian part of Spain during the same period, especially Pedro the Cruel of Castile — was to employ Jews to push unpopular measures.

Almost immediately after coming to the throne, Mieszko III carried out a monetary reform. All the heavy old coins with a high silver content were withdrawn from circulation. In their place thin bracteates, with a silver content one-half to one-third of the old denars, were issued. These new coins were so thin they wore out almost immediately and had to be reissued several times a year. This furnished Mieszko a further opportunity to enrich himself, and the coins grew lighter and more fragile with each new issue. For this purpose the king used Jewish agents, who collected the old coins and brought them to the mint, struck the new coins, and employed other Jews to redistribute them. It should be noted that in this first period of Mieszko III's rule, no Hebrew was engraved on official state money.

After four years, popular resentment reached the boiling point, and the feudal princes, who had been enfeebled by the king, found an opportunity to revolt. Mieszko was overthrown and fled, with Casimir the Just taking over most of his territories.

The new ruler was a weak man, and soon each of the rebellious princes began to issue his own currency, the very policy opposed by Mieszko — and the sole affirmative feature of his monetary reform. Casimir the Just also continued to employ Jewish mint masters. In Cracow he issued only denars with Latin inscriptions; but at Gniezno he struck bracteates, some with Hebrew inscriptions, the first Hebrew to appear on Polish state coins. The most common type is inscribed "Beracha Casi" or "Blessing on Casimir."

General discontent with the resultant economic chaos gave Mieszko another chance. By means of an enormous loan, he raised a large army and retook most of his old territory.

We do not know the source of his financing. But it is noteworthy that immediately after his return to power Mieszko gave a life grant to the Jews for the farming of the Gniezno mint and for control of its yearly exchange. The Jews also became collectors of taxes, keepers of the royal monopolies, and royal judges. They likewise took over the mints in other provinces, which were subsequently annexed. It is not difficult, therefore, to guess at the origin of the loan that brought Mieszko III back to power.

The state coins of Mieszko during his second reign all bear Hebrew inscriptions. The most common type is that inscribed "Beracha" — sometimes augmented, as "Beracha Mszka" or "Blessing on Mieszko," "Beracha Tova" or "Good Blessing," and even "Beracha V'Hatslacha" or "Blessing and Success." Others indicate, likewise in Hebrew, words such as the name of the king and Gniezno, the city of the mint. A few are also stamped with the name of the mint master, such as Yosef.

When Mieszko was compelled to give up part of his rewon territory to his sons, this practice was continued by them. Mieszko the Younger in Kalisch issued bracteates during his short reign with a higher silver content. On them the names of the mint masters appeared in Hebrew, stamped alongside the mint city of Kalisch; we know of ben Yaacov, Yosef, Menachem, and one extraordinary piece with the entire face taken up by the name Rabbi Avraham Bar Yitzhak Nagid.

Bolislaus of Kuiawy, another son of Mieszko III who received territory from his father, also had a short life.

At his mint city of Inowroclaw, he issued attractive bracteates. At first he, too, employed Jewish mint masters but permitted only his own name to be stamped on the coins in Hebrew. Later he switched to inscriptions in Latin.

In the middle part of the 13th century Mieszko III's great-grandson Przemeslaus I took power at Posen. There is evidence that, like his ancestor, he was aided by a large loan from the Jews of Gniezno, which enabled him to reconquer territory overrun by the princes of Silesia. Hebrew then reappeared on the state mintage farmed to Jews, especially the "Beracha" run, with its variants. Also we know of three Jewish mint masters from their stampings, Menachem, Yaacov, and Avraham.

The last Polish ruler to permit Hebrew on state coins was Przemeslaus II, son of the man of the same name. Again the wealth of the Jews of Gniezno was a prime factor in the internal war that brought him to the throne, and in 1278 he occupied all the territory of Great Poland. His gratitude was obvious, for the mint was again restored to the Jews and the "Beracha" series reinstituted. And under his reign appears coinage bare of inscription but adorned with a head of a Jew wearing the typical flat triangular Jewish hat of the period. Thus, official Polish currency was decorated with a Jewish portrait rather than that of the king! Outside of coins issued by the direct descendants of Herod the Great for pagan districts to the north and east of old Judea, this is the first time to the knowledge of the writer that a Jewish portrait appeared on a coin in all history.[63]

To sum up, it can be stated with certainty that for some hundred years, in the 12th and 13th centuries, the official currency of Poland, indeed the only legal tender, was not only issued by Jewish mint masters but had Hebrew inscriptions on the coins. And it should be emphasized that these coins were issued in large quantities; for example, in a single hoard found at Glembokie, in the province of Posen, there were 640 bracteates with Hebrew inscriptions from the reign of Mieszko III.[64]

The close of the reign of Przemeslaus II marked the end of Hebrew on Polish currency. But the Jews still continued to wield great economic influence, especially under King Casimir III the Great and Queen Yadwiga.[65] Jordanis Lewko (or Levko) was court banker to Casimir, who transferred to him the mint of Cracow during the decade of the 1360s, apparently as security against a large loan.[66] Lewko's financial power was so great complaints were addressed to the pope by the nobility without success. Under Sigismund I the Old, an apostate Jew by the name of Abraham Esofowitz – spelled also Ezefovitch – was appointed mint master in 1508. He was also head of the treasury of the grand duchy of Lithuania from 1509 to 1518. Jan Abramowitz, son of Abraham – considered a Catholic – was granted patents of nobility in 1528;[67] there is some indication that the father also received a title of nobility in the last years of his life. Rather curiously, Abraham's brother, Michael, who participated in these various financial enterprises, not only remained Jewish but had a son who held rabbinical office.

Again in 1555 King Sigismund Augustus II in his Lithuanian province of Poland "leased to a certain Jew in Vilna" the privilege of minting coins for three years.[68] In 1560 the Vilna concession was given to two Jews, named Felix and Borodavka;[69] Borodavka received the same concession again in 1569. Jacob Jacobson was a mint lessee for Sigismund III (1587–1632) and Wladislaw IV (1633–1648), first in Bromberg (Silesia) from 1621 to about 1628, and thereafter at Elbing, Danzig, and Thorn until 1639. His mark "I I" on the reverses of ducats, thalers, and half thalers can still be seen.[70] And last, Loewe Mirewicz in 1652 was entrusted with the working of the mint at Oppeln (Silesia).[71]

The case of Breslau is unusual. The city stood at the nexus of German-Polish trade, and its coinage was often in Jewish hands. Under Emperor Charles V, Isaac Meir (or Mayer) from Prague administered the mint from 1546 to 1549.[72] Salomon Lewen served a very long period, first as warden and then as mint master, from

Types of Polish Bracteates by Jewish Mint Masters, 12th and 13th Centuries
Reproduced from Moshe Boné, "Hebrew Inscriptions on Mediaeval Polish Official Coins," **Israel Numismatic Bulletin**, Nos. 3–4 (Aug.–Dec. 1962).

Explanatory Chart for Drawings of Polish Bracteates

No.	Type	Inscription		Diam. mm.
	Casmir the Just, 1177-81			
1.	Bishop holding crozier in left hand	ברכה קזי	Beracha Casi	19
	Mieszko III the Elder, 1181–1202			
2.	Two dukes standing, a sword between	משק	Meshek	21
3.	Faces of the dukes	טובה ברכה	Beracha Tova	21
4.	Above – dragon, below – two doves	ג.נ.ז.ד.ו.	(sic) Gnesdo	21
5.	The king slaying a dragon	הצלת	Hazalat	
6.	The king standing, holding branch	מושל טוב	Moshel Tov	20
7.	On r. – crowned head, on l. lion	משקא — יושף הכהן	Mishka Yosef Hacohen	20
8.	Lion to left	משקו קריל פלסה	Mishko Kril Polsha	20
9.	Legendary bird with outspread wings	ברכה והצלחה	Beracha V'Hazlacha	20
10.	King holding sword	מישקא	Mishka	20
11.	King standing, holding standard	ברכה	Beracha	19
12.	King standing, holding palm-branch	ברכה	Beracha	19
13.	King standing, holding hawk	ברכה	Beracha	19
14.	On r. – king standing, on l. – eagle	ברכה	Beracha	18
15.	Angel with outspread wings	ברכה	Beracha	18
16.	On l. – king, on r. – tree	ברכה	Beracha	18
17.	Two eagles	ברכה	Beracha	18
18.	King seated, holding sword and flower	רב טוב	Rav Tov	17
19.	King holding sword and standard	מישקא	Mishka	17
20.	King standing, holding a sword	ברכה	Beracha	17
21.	King holding water-lily	ברכה טובה	Beracha Tova	16
	Mieszko the Younger, Duke of Kalisch, 1186–94			
22.	Lion standing to left	יוסף קליש	Yosef Kalisch	21
23.	Above dragon, below – two doves	קליש	Kalisch	21
24.	City-gate, within, duke holding sword	יוסף	Yosef	21
25.	City-gate, within, duke holding sword	אברהם	Avraham	21
26.	Eagle to left	ב. יעקב	B. Yaakov	20
27.	Duke seated on throne	קליש	Kalisch	20
28.	Inscription in four rows	יוסף בן יהודה' הכוהן קליש	Yosef Ben Yehuda Hacohen Kalisch	20
29.	Inscription in four rows	מון מנחם מניפיר קליש	Mon Menachem Manifir Kalisch	20
30.	Inscription in four rows	רבי אברהם בר יצחק נגיד	Rabbi Abraham Bar Yizhak Nagid	20
	Bolislaus, Duke of Kujavien, 1186–1195			
31.	Head of the duke	בוליסליו	Between 4 crosses Bolislaw	21
32.	Sheep	בוליסליו	Between 4 crosses Bolislaw	20
	Przemeslaus I, 1242–1252			
33.	King on r., bishop on l.	מנחם	Menachem	18
34.	King on r., bishop on l.	יעקב	Yaakov	18
35.	Head of the king	משקא דוכוס	Mishka Dukus	18
36.	Unidentified design	אברהם היה ברכה	Abraham Haya Beracha	17
37.	Bird sitting on a tree	ברכה טובה	Beracha Tova	16
38.	Tree and flower	ברכה טובה	Beracha Tova	16
39.	Lion to right	קצין ומלך	Kazin V'Melech	16
40.	Head of the king	ברכה והצלחה	Beracha V'Hazlacha	15
41.	Ornamental frame, within, inscription	ברכ(ה) — ברכ(ה)	Berach(a) Berach(a)	15
	Przemeslaus II, 1279–1296			
42.	Head	ברכה	Beracha	15
43.	Head	ברכה והצלחה	Beracha V'Hazlacha	15

Polish Bracteates by Jewish Mint Masters, 12th and 13th Centuries (Numbers refer to line drawings on preceding page.)

No. 1. "Beracha Casi" (Blessing to Casimir)

No. 2. "Meshek" (Mieszko)

No. 12. "Beracha" (Blessing)

No. 14. "Beracha" (Blessing)

No. 16. "Beracha" (Blessing)

No. 16.

No. 14.

Enlargements of the "Beracha" Type

1565 to 1600. He is said to have been arrested in 1583 for issuing light currency; but since he continued in office, either the information is incorrect or he was cleared.[73] And during the Thirty Years War (1618–1648), Manasseh from Hotzenplotz served as the Breslau mint's director.[74]

Although no Jew was allowed high public office in Hungary during this period, Isaac was appointed minter in 1524 at Kashau (Kassa, now in Czechoslovakia) by King Louis II (1511–1526). The document of his appointment on the recommendation of the king's treasurer states that he should be given a place to live and protection despite his being a Jew "because of his rare understanding of the art of minting." The coins struck by Isaac are called "Isaaciden."[75]

Shortly thereafter, starting on April 23, 1566, "The Jew Phybes" from Hanover became lessee of the mint at Wunstorf (Brunswick, in central Germany) under Duke Erich II, the Younger (1528–1584). We do not know how long he retained the post.[76]

A Marrano operating in northern Germany was Samuel Jachia, who called himself Alvaro Diniz (or Dionysius) in the Portuguese Marrano community of Hamburg and Albert Dionis (or Denis) under Danish rule. First noted in 1605 as a rich merchant of Hamburg, he also maintained one of the three local synagogues in his home. Receiving a license to mint coins in Hamburg, he debased the currency and was forced to leave the city, settling in nearby Altona. In 1619 Christian IV of Denmark invited Albert Dionis to move to Glueckstadt, where he became master of the mint for several years. Coins produced at this mint received his special mark, a curious representation of a jar from which lots were drawn, then used for lotteries.[77]

Quite notorious in his time was Lippold (Leupold), originally from Prague, who became both mint master and finance minister in Berlin from 1565 to 1570 under Prince Elector Joachim II of Brandenburg. His story is very similar to that of the celebrated "Jud Suess" almost two centuries later. Lippold, who apparently

Jacob Jacobson (I I)
Mint Lessee at
Bromberg, Elbing,
Danzig and Thorn

Thaler, 1631
Struck at Elbing under King Sigismund III

Thaler, 1637
Struck at Thorn under King Wladislaw IV

Isaac Meir
Mint Administrator at Breslau under Emperor Charles V

3-Groschen Coin, 1546

Silver Denar, 1549

was greedy and lecherous like the Elector, had the full confidence of his master and showed the audacity to mark his currency with a prominent Star of David. But Joachim II suddenly died in January of 1571, by poison it was believed. The rumor spread that Lippold was guilty and unpopular for both his religion and personal character, he was seized by the new Elector Johann Georg and tortured until he "confessed." Thereupon he was racked and quartered,[78] though it may be added that at the end he withdrew his confession and refused baptism.

Albert Dionis
Mint Master at Glueckstadt under Christian IV of Denmark
Mark: Lottery Jar
Thaler, 1623

Court Jews and Coin Jews

The epoch of European Court absolutism, running through most of the 17th and 18th centuries, witnessed a sharp improvement in the economic position of certain favored Jews. This was centered in the Austrian Empire and the other German states. The men were "Hof-Juden" or Court Jews and "Muenz-Juden" or Coin Jews. In many ways similar to their predecessors in the feudal period, these Jews used their skills and a web of family and communal contacts to aid their princes. Some of the relationships became amazingly intimate, while others were formal and cold; but all were characterized by the precarious fact that the Christian prince could dispense with such services at will, often voiding debts and throwing the erstwhile favorite into jail.

The first of these figures appeared in Austria. In 1615 Veit Prod and Abraham Riss, both "freed Court Jews," took over the mint office of Falkenstein when Paul Sixtus, Count of Trautson, came to power. In the following year Prod offered to deliver annually one thousand marks of fine silver to the nearby Viennese mint; we do not know the subsequent history.[79] At Vienna itself, Jacob Bassevi, descended from a well-known family of Prague, became in 1622 one of the members of a trio that leased the imperial mint and debased the currency. Though a national scandal ensued, Bassevi was left untouched because his two

Lippold
Mint Master for Prince Elector Joachim II of Brandenburg, 1565–1570
Mark: Star of David between rosettes
10 Kreutzer (Angel Groschen), 1568

Velt Prod and Abraham Riss
Mint Lessees under Paul Sixtus
Count of Trautson at Falkenstein
Thaler, 1620

partners were Prince Lichtenstein and General Wallenstein (the Jew provided the expertise and the Christians the political contacts). In fact, Emperor Ferdinand II granted him a coat of arms that same year; thus Jacob Bassevi was among the first Jews to be made noblemen.

Shortly thereafter, Israel Wolf, a "freed Court Jew," signed an agreement whereby the business of coining money at the Viennese mint was transferred to him as representative of a Jewish syndicate. The records do not indicate the length of the contract,[80] but it is apparent that Jews had a strong position in Austrian mints at this time. Partly as a reaction, Emperor Leopold I expelled the Viennese Jews in 1670, though he continued to lean heavily on Jewish financiers, such as Samuel Oppenheimer and Samson Wertheimer. In fact, Leopold's chief purveyors for the Imperial Mint were three Jews, Simon Michael, Marx Schlesinger, and Lazarus Hirschel. The last named, whose family for several generations was also involved in supplying ore to the Breslau mint, was appointed mint master in Brieg, near Breslau.[81]

The connection was just as close in the smaller German states. Abraham Juedt of Goldkronach was mint contractor of Gundelfingen and Stockau (Wuerttemberg) in 1622.[82] Daniel Oppenheimer was the mint master at Oettingen (Bavaria) around 1675.[83] And Samuel Levy of Metz (Chief Rabbi of Alsace), as head of a Jewish syndicate, took over the mint of the Duke of Lorraine in 1712.[84]

For a short period, from 1659 to 1660, a Jewish mint master operated at Wischau, in Moravia. A leaseholder of the mint with insufficient knowledge and capital took as a partner Asher Rosi, who issued coins with a Star of David as his mint mark. The ecclesiastical authorities, who had banished Jews from the area, considered this an insult and forced the dismissal of Rosi. There are still extant curious examples of this coinage, which show on one side Archduke Leopold Wilhelm (1637–1662), Archbishop of Olmuetz, while the other

Asher Rosi
Mint Lessee at Wischau, Moravia
Mark: Star of David (bottom of reverse)
15-Kreutzer Coin Showing Archduke Leopold Wilhelm

side is stamped at the bottom with a Jewish star.[85]

The better-known Court Jews, who reached their zenith in the 18th century, had close contacts with the mints. Seligmann Loew and his son in Bavaria, Baruch Hollander at Hesse, and Moses Benjamin Wulff at Gotha and Altenburg all had monopolies on ore shipments to the mints of their rulers.[86] These Court Jews often sold such concessions to other Jews. Through Berlin contacts, for example, Joel Levin became silver supplier in Leipzig (Saxony) in 1719; one source even claims he was mint master there as well.[87] He was followed by Gerd Levi, a relative of Wulff, who was also silver supplier to the Leipzig mint, receiving a flat salary of one hundred thalers. Though he was ordered to leave in 1733, the decree was rescinded, and Gerd Levi continued in that capacity until his death in 1739. Levi Gerd, his son, was immediately appointed successor, with the official title of mint overseer, and worked at Leipzig until his death as a very old man in 1794.[88]

Some of these Court Jews took the mint into their own hands. Moses Benjamin Wulff administered the mint at Anhalt-Dessau. Jacob David of Mannheim leased the mint at Saxe-Meiningen.[89] The most famous was "Jud Suess," Joseph Suskind Oppenheimer, lessee of the Stuttgart mint from March 9, 1734, and financial minister to the Duke of Wuerttemberg. After the duke died, Oppenheimer was seized and hanged in 1738; the event was so celebrated that several medals were struck to commemorate the occasion.

The "Muenz-Juden," or Coin Jews, were particularly strong at the Prussian court.[90] Frederick William, The Great Elector (1620–1688), appointed Israel Aron (or Aaron) as supplier to the Berlin mint and granted the right of striking small coins to Esther, the wife first of Israel Aron and then, after Aron's death, of the court jeweler Jost Liebmann. In this same period, around 1675, Moses of Helmstadt received the monopoly to supply the mint in Stettin (Pomerania).[91] Frederick William I (1688–1740) reluctantly hired Jewish mint suppliers after Christian officials had failed. Levin Veit

Medals of Jew Suess, Lessee of the Stuttgart Mint

The Seizing of Jew Suess, 1738

The Hanging of Jew Suess, 1738
(double size)

furnished all the necessary silver and coined the money under the supervision of a Prussian mint master. After Veit's death, Moses and Elias Gumperts, tobacco manufacturers, took over for a brief period.

Frederick the Great (1740–1786) shared the prejudices of his father but soon found it necessary to lease the state mints to Jews. In 1751 a Jewish firm (consisting of Daniel Itzig, an important banker, his brother-in-law, the money dealer Moses Isaak, and Hertz Moses Gumperts or Gomperz of the tobacco family), contracted for the Breslau mint. In 1755 the firm, known as Itzig, Moses & Co., leased the six state mints. Beaten in the competition was another syndicate formed by the Fraenkel brothers and Veitel-Heine Ephraim, court jeweler to Frederick, which had earlier leased the mints at Koenigsberg and Breslau for several years. In 1758, when Gumperts died and the feud between the two Jewish factions ceased, the firms merged, and the king leased all six Prussian mints and the two Saxon mints to the new company. This syndicate operated them for many years. And finally, Hirsch Simon contracted for the Breslau mint at the end of the 18th century.[92]

Frederick the Great, unlike some of his contemporary reigning colleagues, determined mint policy and insisted on a debasement of the coinage in order to finance his many wars (like Emperor Ferdinand II of Austria more than a century earlier). This brought on much anti-Semitism in the general population. But the practice saved the Prussian state, as Frederick himself admitted. Hugo Rachel, the historian of Frederick and a man not sympathetic to the Jews, wrote: "The general lessees were merely mint contractors and made only an 8 per cent profit on the metal they supplied, while the huge profits made by the mints naturally went to the State and to the war treasury."[93]

The emancipation of the Jews, which received its impetus during the French Revolution and gathered additional force under Napoleon, led to a new political climate. As a result, the close relation of Jews to mints and treasuries vanished with the decline of autocratic princely power. For this reason the last Jewish mint masters are found in backwater areas untouched by the revolutionary thinking. Primary among these was the Crimea, still ruled by the Tartar Khans. The Jewish sect of the Karaites flourished here, and relations with the Tartars were cordial. Samuel ben Abraham, son of a famous scholar, was head of the Karaites and became mint master to the last Khan, Sahib Girei. Treasurer of the realm as well, he held the official title of Aga (High Minister). He was succeeded by his son, Benjamin ben Samuel, in both position and title. When the Crimea was conquered by Russia in 1783, Benjamin ben Samuel – a writer and poet as well as a financier – was permitted to retain his title and also acted as protector of the Karaites to the Russian court.[94]

A similar condition existed in Yemen, where the Jews from time immemorial had had an almost exclusive monopoly in metalworking. Skill in engraving led inevitably to mint matters, and Shalom Ha-Cohen, originally from Iraq, was governor of the Yemen mint during part of the 18th century. Members of the wealthy Badihi family served as minters to the Imams in the next century.[95] Yahya ben Judah Badihi, with his father, operated under the Imam El-Mahidi (1815-1835), who jailed them on false charges. Judah paid a heavy ransom, but the son escaped to nearby Karokaban, where he became a distinguished scholar. This is the last recorded case of a Jewish mint master in the sense of a mint lessee or private beneficiary under an autocrat.[96]

The Economic Significance of Hebrew on Medieval European Coinage

The Jewish mint master was a key figure in the transformation of the barter economy of medieval Europe to a money economy. The 12th and 13th centuries show Jewish mint lessees in almost every European country: in Aragon, Catalonia, Castile, Austria, many German states, Moravia, Hungary, Poland, and possibly England. Jews still controlled mints in the 14th century in various Spanish and German states and in Poland. C. W. Previté-Orton in *The Shorter Cambridge Medieval History* (Vol. I, p. 549) states that it was not until 1300 that the monopoly of the Jews on loans and usury was broken by the Italians. It is apparent that this also applies to the operation of many state mints.

The Jewish role in commerce in the medieval period was so extensive that in Frankish lands the expression used in state documents was "Jews and other merchants." Indeed, the use of Hebrew letters or names on official coins would be difficult to understand unless a good part of this money was circulating almost exclusively among Jews. Up to the time of the Crusades, the Jews dominated the trade between East and West in slaves, silk, furs, perfumes, drugs, and spices – the chief trade items. The Church prohibition of interest made the Jews the sole source of risk capital in feudal society.

The Jewish mint masters also acted as a catalyst in the transformation of medieval society. Since the king took an important percentage of the profits from usury, and the Jewish mint lessee often debased money to pay the king's profit, the king was a significant partner in all transactions, in effect a kind of arch usurer. The king used this profit to put down the lesser lords and extend royal power: a very specific example is the case of Mieszko III of Poland, who, through and with his Jewish mint masters, recovered and extended his power over the rebellious nobles. (An irony of history is that this same Jewish function in Castile and Aragon led directly to their expulsion from Spain.) Thus the Jews played an important role in elevating the king, formerly only the leading feudal lord, to a position of dominance. This was a great step forward in the creation of the modern national state.

From around the middle of the 11th century to the middle of the 14th century, the key three hundred years when Europe was shifting from a barter to a money economy, the Jews were almost the sole capital providers. The activity of the Jewish mint masters, extending from Spain through Poland, is only one indication of their influence, but it is an important one. The secular and ecclesiastical authorities had come to depend on Jewish knowledge of money, Jewish international contacts, and a Jewish reliability free of competing loyalties: Jews were brought into the house of the treasury itself, to get the ore, to issue the money, and turn it over in trade. Their economic influence was enormous; but the records are meager, and in many cases it is only through the Hebrew inscriptions on coins that we even know of their presence.[97]

Jewish Political Power through Money Management

In certain medieval states there was a measure of personal political power tied to this economic power. This was especially true in Moslem countries, where there was less religious prejudice.

Moslem Spain had several such figures. Hasdai ben Isaac ibn-Shaprut, born about 915, commanded many state affairs, apparently including the management of minting and finance, under Abd er-Rahman III, the Great (912–961), whose caliphate of Córdoba extended through all but the northern part of the Iberian peninsula. Similar to Hasdai was Samuel ibn-Nagdela (or Nagrela), who lived from 993 to 1055. Samuel became a vizier in the emirate of Granada in 1027 and, after the elevation of the pleasure-loving Badis al-Muzzaffar, practically ruler of that country. He was succeeded by his son Joseph, whose haughty conduct led him to an early fall. When the Almoravides were summoned from Morocco by the Spanish Moslems in 1066 to check the Christian reconquest, Ali, second caliph of the new dynasty (1106–1143), had three Jews as viziers.

This picture was repeated later in Turkey, where rich emigré Jews from Spain and Portugal settled after the expulsion from the Iberian peninsula. Joseph Nasi was influential at the court of Suleiman II, the Magnificent (1520–1566), and, due to his support of prince Selim – who became Selim II (1566–1574) – was that sultan's favorite and received the title of Duke of Naxos. Not

Hasdai ben Isaac ibn-Shaprut
Mint Manager under Abd er-Rahman III, Caliph of Córdoba, 912–961
Dirhem, 958/959 C.E.

Samuel ibn-Nagdela
Vizier under Badis al-Muzzaffar, Emir of Granada, 11th Century
Dinar

Yakub ben Killis
Minister of Finance under Al-Muizz, Fatimid in Egypt, 953–975 C.E.
Dinar, 975/976 C.E.
(See Note 98)

coincidentally, it was in this period that Jews managed the Turkish mints. Nasi was succeeded by Solomon Ashkenazi, of Italian origin, who retained his great power during the reign of Murad III (1574–1595), the next sultan. Also to be mentioned is Solomon Aben-Jaish, born like Nasi in Portugal, who was named the Duke of Mytilene.[98]

Before the expulsion, the Jews in Christian Spain and Portugal were influential through their control of mints and other financial operations. The most important figures may be briefly noted.

In Portugal, King Diniz (1279–1325) named Judah, the chief rabbi of the country, as minister of finance. King Ferdinand (1367–1387) appointed another Judah as his chief treasurer. The extraordinary Isaac Abravanel started his career as finance minister to Alfonso V (1438–1481).

The Spanish state of Aragon had even more significant figures. The "Rothschild of Aragon" was Judah de la Cavalleria, controller-general of revenues and chancellor of the realm for James I (1213–1276). Pedro III (1276–1285), son of James I, employed Joseph Ravaya as treasurer of all Aragon-Catalonia. Shortly before the expulsion in 1492, Marranos such as Luis de Santangel and Gabriel Sanchez held the highest treasury posts of Aragon.

It can be said that the Jews of Castile ran almost without interruption the finances of that state from its rise to the creation of a single Spanish nation. Starting in the 12th century and continuing up to the expulsion, every significant Castilian king employed Jewish treasurers. The leading figures were: Judah ibn-Ezra, in charge of the royal revenue for Alfonso VII (1126-1157); Çulema (Solomon) and his son Zag de Maleha, both treasurers to Alfonso X, the Wise (1252–1284); Joseph of Écija, chief treasurer to Alfonso XI (1312-1350); the renowned Samuel Halevi Abulafia, chief treasurer to Pedro the Cruel (1350–1369); Joseph Pichon, chief treasurer and controller-general for Henry II (1369–1379); and the fascinating Abravanel family, which for three generations guided royalty in financial matters.

Samuel Abravanel (who was forced into baptism in the massacres of 1391 and assumed the name of Juan Sanchez of Sevilla) started his public career under Henry II and by 1397 was the controller-general of Henry III and the queen's treasurer. His son Judah escaped to Portugal, reassumed Judaism, and became financial advisor to a Portuguese prince. Judah's son, Isaac Abravanel, after serving Alfonso V of Portugal, came to Castile and was soon entrusted by Ferdinand and Isabella (jointly with Abraham Senior, another Jew) with the care of their finances.

It must be emphasized that these men did more than rule the treasury, farm the taxes, and run the mints — in these kingdoms, where feudal grandees warred with each other and their kings over the heads of a groaning peasantry, they actually held together the economic life of the countries.

The rise of national states in Western Europe led to the expulsion of the Jewish populations. Popular enmity, partly religious in base and partly due to envy of individually rich Jews (for the majority of Jews lived as poorly as their Christian neighbors), had been held in check during the feudal period by the lords, who benefited so greatly from the Jewish financial role. But already by the 13th century the Lombards, or "pope's usurers," were swarming into so attractive a situation. Then came the Black Death, wiping out a large part of the population in the middle of the 14th century. The disease was blamed by popular superstition on the Jews, who were expelled or massacred in many communities. The Italian and German usurers took the opportunity to fill the gap. Left by this final catastrophe without any vital economic function, the Jews were expelled, respectively, in the 13th century from England, in the 14th century from France, and in the 15th century from Spain.

The Jews did not fare so badly in the German states, where unification came much later, nor in the Austria of the Hapsburgs, due to the nature of the polyglot peoples, nor in certain states like Poland, where the feudal order never evolved into a modern national state. In these areas Jewish mint masters, called Court Jews and Coin Jews because of an enlarged role, continued to exercise their monetary function. The endless wars, both dynastic and now religious as well, gave them new opportunities, and though it is an exaggeration to state that the Jews created modern capitalism (as has been asserted by persons both for and against that economic system), there is no question that the feudal figure of the Jewish mint master has his counterpart in the successor figures on one hand of the private banker and on the other of the public finance minister.

Jewish Finance Ministers after the French Revolution

The French Revolution changed the European mentality. Under Moslem rule, a Jew could attain tremendous power through economic acumen, but he was always subservient to a despotic sovereign — and what could be bestowed could just as easily be taken away. In pre-19th-century Christian Europe, the Jew was always a pawn, no matter how gilded. But the advent of secular society meant that the Jew was no longer a spiritual alien. The Jewish facility in financial matters, born out of their exclusion from almost all trades in the feudal order except that of putting money to work at interest, was now free to be used on the national level. The movement from Jewish mint masters to Court and Coin Jews, and then to Jewish finance ministers, represents the spirit of different ages. The number of Jews who have directly administered state mints in the 19th and 20th centuries is startling. It may be added that several such persons were converts to Christianity or radicals disdaining all religion, but in all cases noted here a Jewish origin is traceable to either one parent or both parents.

Italy has been graced with an extraordinary number of such figures. The short-lived independent 1848 Venetian Republic (headed by Daniele Manin, whose father

Issued by **Isaac Maurogonato**
Treasury Minister, Venetian Republic
5 Lire, 1848
(obverse)

Henry Morgenthau, Jr.
Secretary of the Treasury, U.S.A., 1934–1945
Medal by **Sinnock**

was of Jewish origin) had Isaac Pesaro Maurogonato (1817–1892) as minister of the treasury. Baron Sidney Sonnino (1849–1922), of Jewish paternity, was Italian minister of the treasury in the period 1893-1896. Luigi Luzzatti (1841–1927) held the treasury post for intervals between 1891 and 1906. (Sonnino and Luzzatti both later became Italian prime ministers.) Leone Wollemborg (1859–1932) was minister of finance in 1901. Carlo Schanzer (born in 1865) held this post from 1919 to 1920. Guido Jung (1876–1949) was finance minister in Mussolini's cabinet during 1932–1935.

Quite a few French Jews have likewise held the top financial post in their country. Michel Goudchaux (1797–1862) was twice minister of finance in the provisional government following the 1848 Revolution. A more prominent figure was Achille Fould (1800–1867), whom Louis Napoleon appointed finance minister from 1849 to 1852 and then again in the period 1861–1867. In the 20th century, Louis-Lucien Klotz (1868–1930) was minister of finance in six different administrations between 1910 and 1920. René Mayer (1895–1972) held this post in 1947–1948, before becoming French premier. Pierre Mendès-France, born in 1907, also later French premier, specialized in financial matters and was an undersecretary to the treasury of the Popular Front government in 1938 (headed by Léon Blum, also a Jew), finance commissioner of Algeria in the Free French movement under General de Gaulle, and then appointed by the general in 1945 to the position of Minister of Economic Affairs. And Michel Debré, who became finance minister when de Gaulle returned to power, though considered an anti-Semite, had a grandfather who was a rabbi.

Three Germans guided the finances of their country in this period. The first was Moritz Ellstaetter (1827-1905), minister of finance of the grand duchy of Baden and then, after the unification of Germany, finance minister in 1888. The second was Bernhard Dernburg (1865–1937), a half-Jew, who held this post in 1919. The third was Rudolf Hilferding (1877–1941), who served as German minister of finance two times, first in 1923 and then in 1928–1929.

Small Denmark is amply represented. Christian Georg Nathan David (1793–1874), a Protestant convert at the age of thirty-seven, was secretary of the treasury in 1864 and 1865. Carl Edvard Cohen Brandes (1874-1931), leader of the Danish Liberal Party, held the post in 1907–1910 and again from 1913 to 1920. The same is true for Henry Gruenbaum, born in 1911, who served from 1965 to 1968.

In Austria, Joseph Redlich (1869–1936), who became a Catholic at age thirty-four, was minister of finance in the last Hapsburg government, which fell after World War I, and then again from 1931 to 1934. In this same period, Pál Szende (1879–1935) was appointed Hungarian minister of finance in the coalition government following World War I, going into exile when the Communists under Béla Kun (by birth, also a Jew) seized power. And Frigyes Koranyi, born Friedrich Kornfeld and son of a convert, was Hungarian finance minister in the 1920s.

During the period immediately following the Bolshevik Revolution the finances of the Soviet Union were administered mainly by persons of Jewish birth. Grigory V. Sokolnikov was commissar for finance from 1922 to 1926. He was immediately followed by Aaron L. Scheinman, who served from 1926 to 1928.

Other scattered figures may be mentioned. Camille Gutt (1884–1971) was Belgian minister of finance from 1934 to 1935 and then from 1939 to the Nazi invasion. Sir Ezekiel Sassoon (1860–1932) served as Minister of Finance in five different Iraqi governments from 1921 to 1925; and S. E. Haskail became the first finance minister in the new kingdom set up at the termination of the British Mandate in 1931. Our own Henry Morgenthau, Jr. (1891–1967) was secretary of the treasury under President Franklin D. Roosevelt from 1934 to 1945. Horacio Lafer (1893–1965) held this post in Brazil from 1951 to 1953. Leopold Lovell, born in 1905, was the only white man in the first cabinet of independent Swaziland and in 1967 was made minister of finance, as well as commerce and industry. The most recent figures are Jose Ber Gelbard, finance minister for the late Juan D. Peron after his return to power in late 1973 in Argentina, and Moises Cohen, holding the same position in neighboring Uruguay.

It is apparent that the Jews, despite their tiny number when counted either absolutely or proportionately to the general population, and disregarding politics of right or left, have had an extraordinary representation in state finances since the French Revolution.

The evidence of these myriad persons, of minters and capital providers and finance ministers, indicates that after the Dispersion, in every age and in every country where they settled, Jews made themselves prominent in financial ways and fostered new economic and hence social development, far out of proportion to their numbers in society. The feudal order, the national state, the era of modern capitalism, the emergence of socialist society, all bear witness to this fact.

Parallel to the evolution of the Jewish moneyer, whose success had been due to skill in engraving, has been the evolution of the Jewish medalist, whose renown derives from the same source. That tradition of metal cutting, which led to Jewish moneyers who in some cases went on to mint affairs, also produced individuals less involved in the commercial side and more drawn to the artistic side of the craft. Though the Jewish religion, especially as interpreted by the Ashkenazi, or German-Polish group, interdicted graven images, the cutting of flat surfaces seemed less serious than those in the round. Thus, the first evidence of Jewish artistic genius came through the back door of metal cutting, in graphic art, and most particularly in the striking of medals from engraved dies. The disproportionate number and high quality of Jewish medalists requires a separate study, which will be undertaken in the next chapter.

II Jewish Medalists

Jewish skill in the medallic art is a natural outgrowth of stone and metal cutting. Pewter, seal, and gem engraving were traditional Jewish crafts in Europe, and these skills were often handed down from father to son through several generations. A Jewish *sigillificus*, or seal maker, is mentioned in Dijon, France, about 1363.[1] Reference is made to Jewish stone engravers in documents dating from the 16th century. In this same period the Italian Renaissance produced a Jewish portrait painter and medalist, Moses da Castellazzo (1467-1527), who plied his trade in Venice, Mantua, and Ferrara; though there is evidence he did a medallion of Ercole I, Duke of Ferrara, no work of his survives. And throughout the 17th century the electoral court of Brandenburg employed a line of Jewish seal engravers.

By the middle of the 18th century this tradition had blossomed into general royal patronage. The Protestant courts of Germany and Scandinavia in the Baltic area depended upon Jewish gem and seal engravers, especially the courts of Mecklenburg-Schwerin, Dresden, Brandenburg, Copenhagen, and Sweden. The same was true in the free city of Hamburg. Some of these engravers, moving into the field of medals, became famous. The most illustrious, Jacob Abraham and his son Abraham Abramson,[2] came out of Prussia. In Denmark, three generations of the Jacobson family were renowned. The beginning of the 19th century saw the spread of this influence. Avenir Griliches in Russia was succeeded by his gifted son, Abraham Griliches. The eminent Belgian gem cutter, Jacob Simon, trained his remarkable son, Jean-Henri Simon; two other brothers, Mayer Simon and Samuel Simon, were also talented, as was Jean-Henri's son, Jean Marie Simon. Another example from Belgium is L. Baruch, uncle of Jacques Wiener, who taught his nephew the art of engraving. Jacques Wiener in turn passed this knowledge on to his two younger brothers, Leopold and Charles. The Elion family in Holland followed the same pattern. Thus, the family tradition of Jews as engravers in stone and metal led directly to their proficiency as medalists.

Jewish Medalists in Germany and Scandinavia

The first medal definitely known to be struck by a practicing Jew is extraordinary in that the engraver, an amateur, was the son of a rabbi, and the subject was likewise rabbinic. In 1735 the Ashkenazi, or German Jewish community, of Amsterdam lacked a rabbi, and the Chief Rabbi of Brody, in Poland, was called to the post. Rabbi Elazar ben Samuel Shmelka accepted, and this medal was struck to celebrate his arrival. The obverse shows a portrait of the rabbi, in contravention of Jewish Ashkenazi tradition at the time, and the reverse is filled with a lengthy inscription in Hebrew. The medalist was Joel, son of Rabbi Lippman Levi, who stamped his name on the reverse. This is the only recorded work of Joel, and from an aesthetic standpoint it must be considered mediocre.

The Jewish court engravers reached their zenith in the second half of the 18th century. Among them, Jacob Abraham and his son, Abraham Abramson, are the most famous. The lives and works of these two men have been recorded in *Jacob Abraham und Abraham Abramson – 55 Jahre Medaillenkunst (1755–1810),* by Tassilo Hoffmann (Frankfurt am Main, 1927). Their activities are briefly noted here.

The father (1723–1800), originally from the German duchy of Mecklenburg-Strelitz, started cutting precious gems at the age of thirteen. His talent was recognized by Frederick the Great, who hired him as a die cutter in 1752 at the Berlin mint, where he had already been working for two years without official status. In 1753 he was transferred, with the title of Royal Medalist, to a new mint set up at Stettin, where he also cut small coins as well as Polish money. This mint was closed down in 1755, and Jacob Abraham was shifted to the Koenigsberg mint. The Seven Years' War (1756–1763) broke out, and Abraham fled before the Russian advance in 1758, being ordered first to Danzig and then

Joel, Son of Rabbi Lippman Levi
First Medal Struck by a Practicing Jew, 1735
Welcome to Amsterdam of Rabbi Elazar ben Samuel Shmelka

to the Dresden mint in 1759, where he made the Bernburger four-and-eight-groschen pieces (equivalent to our dimes) for the war-stricken city. The Russian advance continued, and Abraham was called back to the Berlin mint, where he cut the coin die for a new Prussian eagle on the 1761 thaler piece and also executed a group of medals honoring the rising military fortunes of his king. In the last years of his rather adventurous life Jacob Abraham worked independently, concentrating on medals. Though he neither designed nor modeled, his medals – cut in the style of the late baroque period – became renowned throughout Germany.

There are some three dozen medals of this master listed by Tassilo Hoffmann. Among the best known are those commemorating the victories of Frederick the Great. Also esteemed are his portraits of Major General Paul von Werner and Commandant Heinrich Sigismund von der Heyde, both done in 1760. His outstanding commemorative medals are the 500th Year Celebration of the City of Koenigsberg in 1755 (his first and perhaps best medal), the Marriage of George III of England with Princess Sophie Charlotte of Mecklenburg-Strelitz in 1761, and the Marriage of Wilhelm V of the Netherlands and Princess Wilhelmina of Prussia in 1767. It may be added that Jacob Abraham's powers declined, and he produced little significant work in the last two decades of his life. Of special Jewish interest is the reverse side of the famous Moses Mendelssohn portrait medal (his son engraved the obverse portrait), showing the head of a skull surmounted by a butterfly, which symbolized immortality.

The talents of Abraham Abramson (1754–1811), one of three artistic sons, surpassed even those of his father, Jacob Abraham, whose assistant at the Berlin mint he became at the age of seventeen. In 1782 he was given the title of Royal Medalist. In this period father and son jointly executed medals, the younger man usually doing the portrait side. From 1787 to 1791 Abramson took a long trip abroad, spending most of his time in Italy, where he studied design and modeling. Thereafter he himself modeled his subjects before cutting the dies; he exhibited the heads shaped in wax at the Berlin Academy of Arts, of which he was a member. Abraham Abramson also did iron medallions, and these, with his medals, form a medallic catalog of Berlin personalities of his time. Later in life he turned to coin stamping and in 1809 was responsible for modeling the head of Frederick William III, which appeared on the new Prussian thaler. According to Tassilo Hoffmann, most of the coins struck in Berlin after 1790 were cut by Abramson unless signed by his colleague, Daniel Loos.

Excelling in portraiture, the obverses of Abramson's

500th Year Celebration of the City of Koenigsberg

"Restitution" of Greater Prussia by Frederick the Great

Commandant Heinrich Sigismund von der Heyde

Vaccination Prize Medal, 1805

Frederick William III

Immanuel Kant

Moses Mendelssohn
Intellectual Head of German Jewry
(Jacob Abraham, father, did the reverse.)

Daniel Itzig, Leader of Prussian Jewry

medals are viewed as superior to the reverses, which often are coldly allegoric. As an exemplar of the classical style of the late 18th century, he is considered by many the top medalist of that epoch.

Abraham Abramson's output was enormous, amounting to over 250 pieces, and we can only touch on a small part. Among the series of great men of his time that he executed, those of Kant, Lessing, and Wieland should be noted, as well as the iron medallion of Leibniz. Others are the portrait medals of the three Prussian monarchs he served, Frederick the Great, Frederick William II, and Frederick William III. The wide range of his production includes such medals as the Homage to Czarina Catherine II of Russia in 1783, the Death of Duke Leopold of Brunswick in 1785, the Accession of Czar Alexander I of Russia in 1801, and two famous large medals, the Centennial Celebration of the Prussian Throne in 1801 and the Vaccination Prize medal in 1805.

Abramson put down in metal some of his better-known coreligionists as well, and these are particular gems for the collector of Jewish medals. In chronologic order they are: the portrait of Moses Mendelssohn (with his father cutting the reverse), done in 1774; Daniel Itzig's 70th Birthday, which occurred in 1793; and Dr. Marcus Herz, dating from 1794. Also to be mentioned is the 1808 memorial to the Enfranchisement of the Jews of Westphalia. In 1804 and 1805 Abramson was hired by a Hamburg coin dealer to strike curious Calendar medals, which note the Jewish holidays falling in those years in conjunction with the Christian holidays.

In nearby Copenhagen in this same period the Jacobson family sprang into prominence. The intense Protestant spirit of the Danish monarchs (like those of Sweden) made them sympathetic to the Old Testament: Christian IV often engraved Hebrew on his coins, and a few Jews were even welcome in that country.[3] Aron Jacobson, who was born in 1717 at Wandsbeck and died in 1775 at Copenhagen, became the engraver of the royal seals in 1745. He produced two notable sons. The older, David Aron Jacobson (1753–1812), succeeded his father in the same position. He was also an official die cutter, and his initials, D. I., appear under the head of Christian VII on the speciedaler (a Danish crown) issued at the Altona mint in 1787–1788. But it is the younger son, Salomon Aron Jacobson (1754–1830), who is best known. Though he too cut coin dies (his initials, S. I., appear on the speciedaler of Christian VII issued in 1792 at the Kongsberg mint), his reputation rests on his medallic ability. In 1788 he went to Stockholm, where he became a member of the Academy of Arts. In 1796 he attained the same honor in Denmark. Among his portrait medals may be mentioned several for Christian VII and his successor, Frederik VI; and Count Andreas Peter Bernstorff, a state minister; Georges Cuvier, the French naturalist; Queen Marie Sophie Frederikke; and local notables from Copenhagen, such as Major Generals Christoph Daniel von Kreber and Johan Frederik Classen, Dr. Ole Borch, Dr. Henrik Callisen, as well as the German physiologist, Johan Friederich Blumenbach. Two of his Reformation medals are considered excellent.

Albert Jacobson (1780–1836) was the son of Salomon Aron and the third in this straight line. A member of both the Danish and Swedish Academies of Art, like his father, he was best known for gem engraving. His medallic speciality was prize medals. Few have survived, and the one most frequently cited was struck to honor scientific investigation in the reign of King Frederick VI and shows the portrait of the king. Another known medal is the 1833 issuance celebrating that same king's recovery from a severe illness.[4]

Also noted in this period was the Aaron family. Philipp Aaron was prominent in Mecklenburg-Schwerin, on the Baltic Sea, from around 1747 to 1787. Early in his career we know of a "schautaler" or "display dollar" he struck to celebrate his duke Christian Ludwig II's being given the Russian decoration, the Order of St. Andrew. Issued in 1749, this seems to be the first European Court

Salomon Aron Jacobson

Marie Sophie Frederikke, Hessian Princess

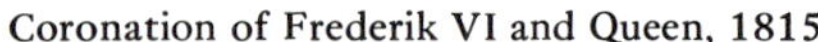
Coronation of Frederik VI and Queen, 1815

Albert Jacobson
Recovery of Frederik VI, 1833

Philipp Aaron
Christian Ludwig of Mecklenburg-Schwerin, Commemorating the Receipt of the Russian Order of St. Andrew, 1749

medal made by a professing Jew. In 1750 he repeated this medal, with slight variations.

He was followed by I. Abraham Aaron (1744–1825), his younger brother, whose first initial I., most likely standing for Jacob, appears only rarely. Abraham Aaron gravitated back and forth between the courts of Mecklenburg and Stockholm, first at Schwerin up to 1776 (where he was assistant to his brother), then in Stockholm from 1776 to 1778, and back again in Schwerin. His best-known piece was issued to celebrate the accession of Great Duke Friedrich Franz I of Mecklenburg, dated 1785. In 1798 he did a similar medal, lauding his duke as a sincere man and good citizen. We know of another medal he struck in 1819 for the Fourth Centennial of Mecklenburg University (the former Rostock Academy), showing the founders Albert and Johann on the reverse, with a portrait of the duke on the obverse. This same duke also commissioned him to do a curious 50th Anniversary medal of Olaus Gerhard Tychsen, Professor of Oriental Languages in Mecklenburg and noted Christian hebraist, which shows both Hebrew and Arabic lettering at the foot of a palm tree. Abraham Aaron was likewise noted for a series of portrait medals of various mayors of Hamburg, namely, Johann Luis in 1788, Johann Anderson in 1790, Martin Dorner in 1798, and Peter Hinrich Widow in 1802. He also did Hinrich Woehrmann, mayor of nearby Luebeck, in 1784.

In Mecklenburg during this same period were the medalists Meier Loeser and his son Nathan. Our knowledge is incomplete, but we do know they lived in Guestrow and in response to a commission in 1793 executed a medal celebrating the Establishment of the Doberan Seaside Resort, that city being a fashionable watering center on the Baltic Sea. The records also indicate that Meier Loeser at the end of the 18th century was called to Sweden by the king in order to cut a coat-of-arms.

Hamburg, somewhat to the west in Germany, was the home city of two 18th-century Jewish medalists. The earlier was Abraham Jacobs, whose first recorded production was the 1765 Jubilee medal for the Hamburg Chamber of Commerce. In 1775 he struck a medal for the Founding of the Hamburg Maritime Insurance Company and in 1778 a portrait medal of the actor Broemann. Jacobs was followed by Abraham Heilbut, born at Hamburg in 1762. Heilbut, trained as a stone cutter and medalist, attracted attention at an exhibition of a trade fair held in Hamburg in 1797. We know of two medals he struck in 1800: a memorial on the death of N. A. J. Kirchhof, a senator from Hamburg; and a 25th anniversary piece for E. J. and Catharine Luebbe, commissioned by their children. There are also two medals with the initials A. H. H., presumed to stand for "Abraham Heilbut Hamburg," both struck to honor mayors of Hamburg: the first, from 1800, for Jacob Albrecht von Sienen; the second, from 1801, for Franz Anton Wagener. A bit more problematic is a medal in similar style, with the initials A. H., struck in 1807 to honor Johann Adolph Poppe, also a mayor of Hamburg. Thus, it would seem that all the mayors of Hamburg from 1788 through 1807 were memorialized by either Abraham Aaron or Abraham Heilbut.

The only Jew to work in Central Germany at this time was Christian Lebrecht Schild (1711–1751), who, as the added first name indicates, converted to the Protestant faith at the age of twenty. Schild, born at Harburg in Swabia, was employed at the mint of Frankfort on Main, doing some sculpture and seal cutting as well. He signed S., C. S., C. L. S., or his full name on coins and medals. In 1741 Schild cut a medal on the forthcoming election of the next Holy Roman Emperor, the inscription expressing the hope he would be a Solomon in judgment. In 1742 he cut the obverses of the double and quadruple ducats issued at Frankfort to celebrate the election of Emperor Charles VII – a reduction of the former was also issued the same year as a proclamation medal. He likewise cut the ducat issued in 1749 at that city. In 1744 Schild did an attractive medal of Johann Friedrich Karl, Count of Ostein and Archbishop of Mainz. An undated medal, issued around 1740 and entitled "Prosperity of the City of Frankfort" is so

I. Abraham Aaron

Accession of Duke Friedrich Franz I of Mecklenburg, 1785

Johann Luis, Consul of Hamburg (Mayor), 1788

Fourth Centennial of Mecklenburg University, 1819

Abraham Jacobs

Jubilee of the Hamburg Chamber of Commerce, 1765

Founding of the Hamburg Maritime Insurance Company, 1775

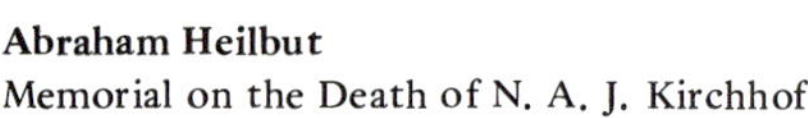
Abraham Heilbut
Memorial on the Death of N. A. J. Kirchhof

Christian Lebrecht Schild

Frankfort on Main Ducat of 1749

Prosperity of the City of Frankfort, c. 1740

Johann Friedrich Karl
Count of Ostein, Archbishop of Mainz, 1744

highly regarded it was among the seventeen chosen by the Historical Museum of Frankfort in 1964 to illustrate the medallic history of the city.[5]

The Russian Jew Judin

Though unlikely in view of the oppressive conditions, it would seem that one of the leading 18th-century medalists was a Russian Jew, by origin if not practice.[6] Samuel Judich Judin, spelled Camoila Iodich Iodin in direct phonetic translation, is a person of whom we know little, partly due to the destruction of the archives of the Russian mints. He was born in 1730; one source states at Moscow and another at St. Petersburg. Possessing extraordinary talent, Judin was accepted at the age of eleven into the School of Engraving of the Moscow Mint. In 1751 he went to St. Petersburg. From 1757 he was listed as an engraver at the St. Petersburg Mint, and in 1762 he and Timothy Ivanov were jointly elevated to head that mint. Judin was last reported as pensioned in 1800.

Samuel Judin did two rubles. In 1757 or 1758 he engraved the obverse of the ruble of Czarina Elizabeth I (following the pattern of Dassier), which he signed on the bottom. In 1762 he also did the obverse of the ruble of Peter III; the limited issue showing his initials C. I-O on the sleeve is today a coveted numismatic item.

Judin has many medals to his credit that, similar to the rubles, were often jointly done with T. Ivanov. In 1758 he struck the Prize Medal of the University of Moscow, in 1770 the reverse of the Award Medal for the Battle of Chesmen, in 1774 the obverse of the 50th Anniversary of the Academy of Sciences, in this same year the obverse of the medal celebrating Peace with Turkey, in 1784 the reverse of Free Trade in Chersones, Feodosie and Sebastopol, and in 1790 the obverse of the Peace Treaty with Sweden. Undated are his Award Medal of the Educational Institute and the Founding of the Imperial Order of St. Andrew (struck from the original dies in the middle of the 19th century).

Judin also was responsible for commemorative medals looking back to momentous events during the reign of Peter the Great. His best-known medal is the Battle of Poltava, which celebrated the Russian victory over Charles XII. Similar to this is his medal commemorating the Annihilation of the Strelitz Guards. Judin likewise copied many medals, following contemporary models sometimes and other times older models; often the details were so altered that a new medal resulted. Foremost among these are the medals commemorating Count Peter Shuvalov and Peter the Great's Birth and Inauguration.[7]

Transition to the 19th Century: Jean-Henri Simon

The giants of the 18th century had their equals in the 19th century. The transitional figure was Jean-Henri Simon, whose long and adventurous life extended from 1752 to 1834. Son of the noted seal engraver and gem cutter, Jacob Mayer Simon,[8] he was born in Brussels and learned the trade in childhood. As early as 1767 he was working as a gem engraver for Prince Charles of Lorraine. Eight years later he went to Paris and found employment with the Duke of Chartres, later Duke of Orleans. Louis XVI then granted him the title of Royal Engraver, with apartments in the Louvre gallery. He held the position until 1792, when this picaresque personality joined the forces of the French Revolution. Within a short time Simon became a lieutenant-colonel in the army of the French Republic. Falsely accused of treason, he fled France and entered employment as an engraver to the court of Spain. He returned with the advent of Napoleon, rejoined the army, and became a full colonel of a regiment of lancers. Twice wounded, he finally quit the military service and was appointed an engraver to the Cabinet of Napoleon; he also had the official position of Engraver of Title Seals to the Empress Josephine. Like the phoenix, he returned to Brussels after the fall of Napoleon and became Engraver to King William I of the Netherlands, who then

Samuel Judin

The Founding of the Imperial Order of St. Andrew under Peter the Great
(Date of 1698 is date of founding, not of medal.)

Russian Ruble, 1762
St. Petersburg Mint
Peter III (obverse)

Anna, Empress of All Russia
(Portrait copied from J. C. Hedlinger's 1735 medal. Date of 1730 is date of coronation, not of medal.)

Jean-Henri Simon

Inauguration of the New Harbor at Middleburg, 1817

Frederica Louise Wilhelmina, Queen of the Netherlands, 1820

King William I of Belgium and the Netherlands, 1820
(obverse)

Rembrand van Rhyn, c. 1820
(obverse)

ruled over Belgium as well. The last curious episode of Simon's life occurred when, at the age of seventy-eight, he took command of a company of Civic guards on the outbreak of the 1830 Revolution at Brussels.

The gem engraving of Simon has received considerable attention because his skill was so great; the cameos and intaglios were often mistaken for those of antiquity. But the range of his medallic production is also noteworthy. The Hague Museum has a fine collection of some two dozen of his medals. The most important persons engraved were William I and the Queen, Crown Prince William, Prince Frederick, and Princess Marianne of the Netherlands; he also did prize medals for the Universities of Leyden, Utrecht, Groningen, Liege, and Louvain.

Simon's most important work is his series of 100 medals of illustrious men of the Low Countries, on which he spent six years of constant labor. Uniformly measuring almost 2 inches in diameter, they include such figures as Erasmus, Hugo Grotius, Gerard Mercator, Quentin Metsys, Lucas of Leyden, Peter Breughel the Elder, Peter Paul Rubens, Anthony Van Dyke, Rembrandt, David Teniers, Egmont, and William of Orange.

Though Jean-Henri was the finest flower of the Simon family, there were other important members as well. Mention has been made of Jacob Simon, his father. Mayer Simon (1746–1821), better known as Simon de Paris, a brother of Jean-Henri, built a reputation on gem portraiture, having engraved such persons as Louis XVI and Napoleon. Another brother, Samuel Simon, born 1760, was engraver to the Parisian post office. The line continued an additional generation through Jean Marie Amable Simon, son of Jean-Henri. Although the son did not inherit the genius of his father, he was a talented gem engraver and had a distinguished career of portrait engraving under the French Restoration and King Louis Philippe.

The Wieners of Belgium

Belgium produced several other extraordinary Jewish medalists in the 19th century. The first, L. Baruch, had a career that overlapped that of Jean-Henri Simon. But Baruch's most significant contribution was the training of his nephew, Jacob Wiener, later called Jacques, with whom he jointly signed some medals in the early days. This Wiener was the oldest of three brothers, all destined for medallic fame.

Jacques Wiener (1815–1899), born in the Rhine province of Hoerstgen of Hungarian immigrants, was placed at the age of thirteen with his uncle, under whom he studied drawing and engraving. At the age of thirty Wiener conceived the idea – rarely before implemented – of engraving in precise detail the exterior and interior of a monument on the obverse and reverse of a medal. He engraved ten medals of famous Belgian churches with extraordinary delicacy. Success was immediate. This feat was then followed by a series of 41 medals, issued between 1850 and 1865, illustrating the most important European buildings, mainly in Germany, France, Italy, and England. By 1866 he had received the highest awards from several of these countries. It should also be noted that Jacques Wiener engraved the first Belgian postage stamps and for many years was head of the government factory issuing these stamps.

In the vast production of this master there are several medals of special Jewish interest: the 1841 Opening of the Jewish Home for the Aged in The Hague; the 1841 Dedication to King William II of the Maastricht Synagogue; a Limburg Jewish Community Award to S. Bloemendal in 1851; and the most noted, the 1861 Grand Opening of the Synagogue at Cologne.

Leopold Wiener (1823–1891), studied with his older brother, Jacques, and then went to Paris, where he became a pupil of the famous David d'Angers. In 1847 he returned home and started engraving for the Belgian mint; he was appointed First Engraver in 1864, a post he held till his death. He was responsible for some of the currency of Leopold I and all coins issued by Leopold II – some 150 pieces are to his credit. Some of these are renowned by numismatists, such as the 5-

Jacques Wiener

Lincoln Cathedral

Grand Opening of the Cologne Synagogue, 1861

Westminster Abbey

franc crown he designed and engraved for Leopold I, issued from 1849 to 1853 and reissued in 1858 and 1865; the commemorative coin, nominally valued at 5 francs, struck to celebrate the marriage of the Duke of Brabant, later Leopold II, in 1853; the new 5-franc crown designed for Leopold II when he ascended the throne in 1865; and the obverse (his brother Charles Wiener, with E. Devaux, did the reverse) of the commemorative coin, again with a nominal value of 5 francs, issued in 1880 to herald the 50th anniversary of the Belgian kingdom.

While First Engraver of the Belgian mint, Leopold Wiener continued to strike medals. A very important project was a series of historical medals on a large scale, most of them being nearly 3 inches in diameter. They commemorated contemporary events and became very popular. This extraordinary man also had a considerable reputation as a sculptor, and several of his monumental works still adorn public places in Belgium. Like his older brother, he garnered top awards from many countries.

The list of Leopold Wiener's medals fills three pages in Forrer's *Biographical Dictionary of Medallists.* They are of all categories – architectural, portrait, award – and also include many jettons. One item of special Jewish interest is his 1859 portrait medal of Henri Loeb, Grand Rabbi of Belgium.

The third and youngest of the Wieners, Charles Wiener (1832–1888), had the shortest life span but perhaps the most brilliant career. He studied first at Brussels and then went to Paris as a student of Oudiné, a founder of the modern school of medalists. As early as 1856 he settled at The Hague and became an engraver to the king of Holland. He then proceeded to London, where he was appointed assistant engraver at the Royal Mint. After a short stay, this restless man went to Lisbon as chief engraver of the Portuguese coins, though as a teacher rather than as a die cutter. Returning to Brussels in 1867, he then devoted himself to medals. Like his brothers, he received top awards from many countries.

An almost complete series of Charles Wiener's medals is held at the Bibliothèque royale of Belgium. They are far too numerous to name here. Quite a few are archi-

Leopold Wiener

Leopold I, King of the Belgians
5 Francs, 1849

Leopold II, King of the Belgians
5 Francs, 1868

Henry Loeb
Grand Rabbi of Belgium

tectural medals, showing churches and state buildings, many done in conjunction with his brother Jacques.[9] Also very common are portrait medals of royalty and exhibition medals. English pieces are foremost among those that have withstood the test of time, such as the portrait medal of Prince Albert, consort of Queen Victoria; the City of London medal; the Commemoration of the Visit of Czar Alexander II to London in 1874; and the Donation by Queen Victoria of Epping Forest in 1882. The last two items are in the collection of the New York Metropolitan Museum of Art. Of special Jewish interest are two portrait medals: the magnificent E. A. Astruc, Chief Rabbi of Belgium, and a dual portrait of Sir Moses and Lady Judith Montefiore.

Russian Medalists of the 19th Century

Although the Wieners of Belgium were the foremost Jewish medalists of the 19th century, there were many others as well whose reputations are well known. Among these are Avenir and Abraham Griliches (also spelled Grilikhes), a father and son considered Russian though both were born in Vilna, Lithuania. The father, Avenir Girschevich Griliches (1822–1905), was self-taught and came to the attention of the Russian court by engraving a striking resemblance of the czar. In 1871, rather late as these careers go, he was employed as an independent engraver by the Imperial Mint of St. Petersburg – in fact, he was one of the few Jews permitted to stay in St. Petersburg at this period.[10] In 1889 and 1898 he is listed officially as a mint engraver, though earlier, in 1874, he was already nominated to the St. Petersburg Academy of Fine Arts. His mark was his initials "A. G." in the Cyrillic script. Avenir Griliches is credited with engraving the state seals of the czars Alexander III and Nicholas II. In 1886, when Alexander III reformed the coinage, he engraved the reverse side of the new money, showing the Imperial Russian eagle, and the design was used on the reverses of the rubles and kopecks throughout the reign of this czar. In 1898 Avenir Griliches engraved the commemorative ruble for

Alexander II, issued by Nicholas II. He received top Russian honors, including decoration with the Order of St. Stanislas and appointment as a court Councilor, a position that automatically ennobled him.

The son, Abraham Avenirovich Griliches (1852–1912), had an even more celebrated career. Graduated from the St. Petersburg Academy of Fine Arts in 1876, he was hired as an engraver to the Imperial Mint. In 1886, when his father engraved the reverse for the new coinage, the son won the competition depicting the portrait of the new czar, which likewise graced the obverses of the denominations until the death of Alexander III. In the early 20th century Abraham Griliches was elevated to principal mint engraver at the St. Petersburg Mint and is credited with the dies for the obverses of the coins of Nicholas II, as well as the commemorative ruble for Alexander III issued by Nicholas II in 1912. But Abraham Griliches was even more noted for his medals and gem engraving and took top awards at the Paris Expositions in 1889 and 1900.

Charles Wiener

Visit of Czar Alexander II to London, 1874 (obverse)

Rabbi E. A. Astruc

Sir Moses and Lady Judith Montefiore (obverse)

Avenir Griliches

Russian Ruble, 1898
Alexander II Commemorative
(similar to a 78 mm medal issued the same year)

The Jubilee of the Moscow Stock Exchange, 1889
(reverse)

Centenary of the Mining Institute, 1873
(reverse)

It is difficult to distinguish between the medals of father and son because their initials were the same and they both struck medals in the same period: for a medal signed "Griliches," distinction is impossible except by outside reference.[11] Since Russian custom makes the father's name the middle name of the son, when signed "A. G. G." the medal is done by the father, and when signed "A. A. G." the medal is done by the son. Also, aware of the difficulty, Avenir Griliches sometimes added "Father" after his name, while Abraham Griliches often added "Son." There is still, however, an area of doubt with certain medals.

The important medals of the father are: the reverse side of the 1872 50th Anniversary of Minister K. V. Tchevkine; the reverse side of the 1873 Centenary of the Mining Institute; the 1888 Opening of the University of Tomsk; the 1889 Jubilee of the Moscow Stock Exchange; and the undated enormous Prize Medal of the Ministry of Transportation for Railroad Schools. Since Avenir Griliches' talent ran more to representing buildings and

Abraham Griliches

Russian Ruble, 1912
Alexander III Commemorative

Commemoration of Death of Czarina Maria
Alexandrowna, 1880 (obverse)

Prize Medal for Racing

monuments than to portraits, he sometimes — and especially in the early part of his career — engraved only the reverse of medals.

The more renowned medals of the son (aside from various pieces showing the busts of the czars) are: the obverse of the 1880 Commemoration of the Death of Czarina Maria Alexandrowna; the 1883 Commemoration of the Construction of the Transcaucasian Railway; the 40th Anniversary, falling in 1887, of Professor V. L. Gruber, a revered teacher of the sciences; the 1887 50th Anniversary of the mineralogist N. I. Koksharov; the Commemoration of the Saving of the Lives of the Czar's Family at the Railway Disaster of Borki in 1888; and Count Nicholas Max.Romanovski, Duke of Leuchtenberg, done in 1890. Abraham Griliches also did quite a few prize medals for agricultural and racing groups, and his representations of horses are excellent. It might also be mentioned that an early self-portrait dates from 1870.

The Smithsonian Institution's Museum of History and Technology, located in Washington, D.C., has a magni-

Abraham Griliches

Count Nicholas Max. Romanovski, Duke of Leuchtenberg, 1890 (obverse)

ficent collection of medals by both Griliches. Included are two of Jewish interest, both probably by the son when judged stylistically. A silver medalet from 1894 shows the bust of Anton Rubinstein, obviously in memoriam since the reverse shows a mourning angel beside a piano. More important is an 1888 silver medal honoring Sam S. Poliakov, an important counselor to Alexander III; rather than concealing his origins in a country where anti-Semitism was rife, Poliakov linked a studying child with a railroad by means of the Shield of David, proudly indicating the motivating force through which the child became a railway magnate.

Related in background and activity to the Griliches was Ilya Guenzburg (1859–1939), born Elias Ginzburg in Vilna, Lithuania. At the age of ten his attempts to sculpt came to the attention of Avenir Griliches, living in that city at the time, who recommended him to the famous Russian Jewish sculptor, Mark Antokolski. The latter took the boy back with him to St. Petersburg, where great talent combined with good looks and charm

Sam S. Poliakov, 1888

Ilya Guenzburg

50th Anniversary of the Society for the Spreading of Education among Jews in Russia (1863–1913)

opened many doors. In 1886 Guenzburg graduated from the St. Petersburg Academy of Fine Arts, and a cultured figure in the artistic and social world of Russia of that time, he became an academician in 1911 and then a professor in 1921 at the academy. Winner of silver and gold medals while a student at the academy and winner of a gold medal in sculpture at the 1900 Paris Exposition, Guenzburg was a society sculptor and medalist. His medals and plaques read like a bibliography of late 19th-century Russian culture. He sometimes collaborated with A. Zhakar, who engraved while he designed, and sometimes worked alone. His most prominent works are: the writers Leo Tolstoy and V.V. Stasov; the painter J. E. Ryepin; the composer N. A. Rimsky-Korsakov; the singer Feodor Chaliapin; the architect P. J. Syuzor; the numismatist K. K. Gil; Count I. I. Tolstoy; Countess Ludmila Tolstoy; and, of Jewish interest, the 50th Anniversary (1863–1913) of the Society for the Spreading of Education among Jews in Russia. A portrait medal of the archaeologist V. R. Rozen might also fall in the Jewish interest category, judging by the name. Ilya Guenzburg wrote several autobiographical works, which are a *Who's Who* for the Russia that died with the Revolution.

A contemporary is Russian medalist Zelig Lerner, presumed to be Jewish by his name. Born in 1909 at Ostrog in the Ukraine, Lerner settled in Moscow after serving in World War II. A graduate of the Moscow Institute of Applied and Decorative Arts, he has since designed medals for the Cultural Ministry of the U.S.S.R. His specialty is portraiture, and a series of his medals honoring celebrated Russian figures includes the poet M. J. Lermontov, the writer D. A. Furmanov, the composers Glinka and Tchaikovsky, and the theatrical teacher and director K. Stanislavsky. Following the style set by official Soviet policy, his work is in the 19th-century realistic tradition.

Several other contemporary Russian medalists may be presumed to be Jewish by their names. They are I. D. Brodsky, A. Feidish, I. L. Levin, P. Shapirov, Z. Shklar

Zelig Lerner
The Agrobiologist I. V. Miciurin

and Sh. M. Zicherman. The last-named seems quite prolific in his production.

French Medalists of the Late 19th Century

The French were the masters in the art of medal making during the 19th century, and among them were several Jews who attained some renown in the second half of the century. The earliest was René Stern, whose firm stamp "Stern, Paris" was familiar in the die-cutting and seal-engraving trade. Stern also served as a court engraver to Napoleon III. His most noted medals[12] are: the Company of the Russian Railways, done in 1858; the Opening of the Railway Line from Paris to Orleans, dated 1859; a commemorative for the Loge Anglaise of Bordeaux; Cholera at Amiens; and, from 1869, the Prince Imperial. Of special interest to Jewish collectors is the prize medal he issued for the Société J. R. Pereire in 1878.

Emile-Arthur Soldi (sometimes listed as Soldi-Colbert) was a more significant medalist than Stern. A Dane by ancestry, his real name being Soldyck, he was born in Paris in 1846 and died at Rome in 1906. At the age of twenty-three Soldi received the Grand Prix de Rome in medal engraving, and he was made a knight of the Legion of Honor when only thirty-two. An amazingly talented man, Soldi was an archaelogist and sculptor as well as a medalist; he was also noted in his time as a writer and translator from Danish. In fact, Ernest Babelon the top French art critic, wrote that Soldi would have become one of the greatest medalists of modern times if he had not scattered his energy in so many different fields.

The best-known medal of E.-A. Soldi is his Memorial to the Victims of the Invasion, referring to the 1870-1871 German victory over France. This medal is still being issued by the French Mint. Other noted commemoratives are: the Reconstruction of Paris, 1876; Homage to Beethoven, 1876; the Centenary of the Birth of Bolivar, 1883; the 50th Anniversary of the Invention of Photography, 1889; and the Association of the Students of Paris, 1892. Soldi also did many portrait medals, including those of the Duchess Colonna de Castiglione, Bernardina Gismondi, and Henriette de Belfort. Roger Marx, inspector general of the French Museums of Beaux-Arts, thought so much of Soldi he included among his illustrations in *Les médailleurs contemporains* (Paris, 1898, Plate XXX) an allegorical medal by Soldi representing Charity.

A figure in many ways similar to E.-A. Soldi in his Renaissance outlook and capacities was Zacharie Astruc (1839–1907), who was born at Angers but spent most of his life in Paris. Astruc was at various times a sculptor, medalist, painter, and author, and he seemed to do all with equal facility. His reputation rested mainly on his literary works and sculpture. As to the first, he authored novels, short stories, plays, art criticism, and poetry – in both French and Spanish. Rather improbably, considering his religion, Astruc at the age of thirty-five was commissioned to make a reproduction of the famous

René Stern
Voyage of Their Imperial Majesties to Auxerre, 1866
(obverse)

statue of St. Francis of Assisi, which had been jealously guarded in the shrine of a monastery at Toledo. The faithful model of Alonzo Cano's masterpiece has been copied so much since then that it is one of the most popular art reproductions in history. Astruc was named a chevalier of the Legion of Honor for his busts and statues, which are in many French public institutions. His portrait medals were popular, and one, of a young girl, was also worthy of illustration in Roger Marx's *Les médailleurs contemporains.*

The French sculptor Emmanuel Hannaux (often spelled Hanneaux) also deserves mention. Born at Metz in 1855, he attended the Ecole des Beaux-Arts of Paris. In 1880 he obtained first mention of the Second Grand Prix de Rome. A knight of the Legion of Honor, his sculpture is in many French museums. It was only in later years that Hannaux took to medal engraving. The Luxembourg Museum has on exhibit a sampling of his work that includes portrait medals of the painters J. J. Henner and Sebastien le Clerc, as well as Mgr. Dupont des Loges, Bishop of Metz. Hannaux specialized in medallic compositions akin to his sculpture, and the Luxembourg also exhibits Mercury and Bacchus, Nereids, an Idyll, and an allegory of Love and Music. Of special Jewish interest are two portrait medals, those

Emile Soldi
Memorial to the Victims of the Invasion, 1870–1871

Emmanuel Hannaux
Narcisse Leven, President of the Jewish Colonization Association (obverse)

of Dr. L. Dreyfus-Brisac, a well-known French physician, and the exceptional study of Narcisse Leven, French president of the Jewish Colonization Association; a portrait plaquette of Coralie Cahen, the French philanthropist; and a commemorative, the 1910 issue for the 50th Anniversary of the Alliance Israélite Universelle.

The last three "Frenchmen" to be named here fit the category only because they spent most of their creative years in France. The first is Samuel Friedrich Beer, who lived from 1846 to 1912. Of Moravian birth, Beer was closely linked with Theodor Herzl and the Zionist movement. Beer is renowned as a sculptor, and his pieces were acquired by the Berlin National Gallery, the Metropolitan Museum of Art in New York City, and the Museum of Fine Arts in Budapest. Though medals were incidental to his career, he engraved the Commemoration of the 1898 Second Zionist Congress, which may be considered one of the most important Jewish medals ever struck. The Metropolitan Museum of Art also has in its collection a large medallion, 27 inches in diameter, of Michelangelo, a very expressive modeling.

The second Frenchman by adoption is Israel Rouch-

Samuel Friedrich Beer
Commemoration of the 1898 Second Zionist Congress

omovsky, a goldsmith and medalist brought up in Odessa, Russia. Rouchomovsky gained worldwide notoriety at the turn of the century as the maker of the "Tiara of Saitaphernes," which was purchased as an important work of antiquity by the Louvre Museum. He was called to Paris to explain the spurious work and settled in that city. At the Paris Salon of 1904 to 1906 he exhibited reliefs and plaques in the repoussé manner. In 1906 he did a portrait medallion of Zadoc Kahn, Grand Rabbi of France. A plaquette dedicated to Max Nordau and several baroque "shaddai" amulets are also to his credit.

The third Frenchman by adoption is Leopold Bernstein-Sinaieff, born in 1867 in Vilna, Lithuania, and killed by the Nazis in 1944. After emigrating to Paris at the young age of fourteen, he distinguished himself as a sculptor, specializing in bronze and marble busts. Bernstein-Sinaieff was made a chevalier of the Legion of Honor in 1901. Rather late in his career he became interested in portrait medals, of which the most noted is the study of Eugene Manuel, the French Jewish poet, which was exhibited at the 1907 Paris Salon.

Aaron Kohn
Circumcision Medal, 1838

Other Jewish Medalists of the 19th Century

Germany, the homeland of the top Jewish medalists in the 18th century, was of less importance in the succeeding century. Though we know of four such men operating in this period, not one of them is of great significance.[13] The earliest, Aaron Kohn, is perhaps the most interesting due to the fact that he was among the very first Jews who did only Jewish themes, with the medals engraved in Hebrew. In 1817 Kohn struck a Tashlikh prayer medal, which relates to a special ceremony practiced on the Jewish New Year. Around this same year he did a similar Tashlikh medal, with a prayer to protect travelers engraved on the reverse. Also quite common, in both silver and bronze, is an excellent circumcision medal, dated 1838, with texts on both sides from the attendant ceremonial. Kohn likewise did Jewish folk amulets, one of which is in the collection of the Jewish Museum of New York.

Isaac Nathan
Jubilee of Chief Rabbi Isaac Bernays of Hamburg, 1847

Isaac Nathan, the next German medalist in chronology, was a partner in Nathan Brothers of Hamburg, a firm of die-sinkers. Apparently, Isaac Nathan was the firm engraver, though the collective "Nathan Bros." was the usual stamping. The Nathan Brothers made medals for the local Hamburg trade over a span of more than thirty years. The author has noted the following: the 1842 Golden Wedding of Mayor Abendroth; the 1862 Hamburg Insurance Company Award Medal for Praiseworthy Ship Captains; the 1863 Prize Medal of the Hamburg Rifle Shooting Society (reissued in 1864 and 1866); the 1868 Commemoration for the Royal Prussian Councillor David Friedrich Weber (designed by Ed. F. Weber, his son); the 1870 Hamburg issue devoted to the hospital-wounded at Christmas (a product of the Franco-Prussian War); and the 1876 Award Medal of the Luebeck Chamber of Commerce. The firm is noted for two medals of some Jewish importance: an 1841 commemorative struck to honor Sir Moses and Lady Judith Montefiore; and the 1847 Jubilee of Chief Rabbi Isaac Bernays of Hamburg.

J. W. Loewenbach
The Inauguration of the New Synagogue at Munich, 1826 (obverse)

J. W. Loewenbach (who stamped his name with the classical "I" for *J*) was a medalist working in Munich from the 1820s through the 1860s. His themes were nationalist, or more precisely, Bavarian. Among his better-known medals are the 1850 Inauguration of the Statue "Bavaria" at Munich; the Seventh Centenary of Munich, done in 1858; and the 50th Anniversary of the Munich October Festival in 1860. Loewenbach also did one of the earliest known synagogue medals, the Inauguration of the New Synagogue at Munich in 1826.

The fourth German medalist, Heinrich Oppenheim of Frankfort on Main, is probably the best known. H. Oppenheim (a nephew of the well-known painter, Moritz Oppenheim) was an engraver of seals, coats-of-arms, and medals. Two of his medals have achieved some renown, the Visit of William I to Frankfort in 1877 and the gold medal struck in that city in 1899 to celebrate the 150th Anniversary of Goethe's Birth. Three other medals may be of interest to the Jewish collector: the memorial to

Heinrich Oppenheim
Ludwig Boerne Death Memorial

Heinrich Oppenheim
150th Anniversary of Goethe's Birth, 1899

the famous baptized journalist, Ludwig Boerne; the Founding of a Home for Lodge XX, No. 372 of B'nai B'rith at Frankfort in 1902; and a presentation to President Madame J. Bloc of the Luxembourg Association for the Israelite Poor.

An early Austrian fits into this study,[14] Ascher Wappenstein of Vienna, who lived from 1780 to 1852. A document of 1821 in the Vienna Mint Archives points him out specifically as a clever artist in die engraving. Wappenstein's best-known medal was a commemorative struck to celebrate the Peace of Paris in 1814. This portrayed the three Allies, Emperor Franz I of Austria, Czar Alexander I of Russia, and King Frederick William III of Prussia. Other portrait medals were his Death of Kosciusko, done in 1819; the chemist Ignaz Fonberg; and the Austrian Crown Prince, later to become Emperor Ferdinand.

The Dutch contributed several good medalists in this period. The earliest was M. C. de Vries, Jr., born at Amsterdam in 1807. Apprenticed to his father, of whom we know little, de Vries then studied die engraving with Jean-Henri Simon. Noted first as a gem engraver, the artist was elected to the Amsterdam Royal Academy of Fine Arts in 1837. Among his medals at The Hague Museum are a Memorial to King William I, 1843; a similar piece for King William II, 1849; the Drainage of the Harlem Sea, 1852; Construction of the State Railways, 1860; the 50th Anniversary of Dutch Independence from France, 1873; and a portrait medallion of General Pieter Pietersen Heyn. Although there is some confusion of M. C. de Vries, Jr., with another medalist of similar name, we are certain he struck an 1832 medal on the Defense of the Citadel of Antwerp and a portrait of Professor Th. van Sminderen. Like all Dutch artists, de Vries looked to Rembrandt, and in 1852 he tried his hand at a small portrait medal, followed in 1873 by an unusually large one, similar to a medallion, with a reproduction of Rembrandt's famous painting *The Night Watch* on the reverse. The last known production of this artist, who issued medals for almost

Ascher Wappenstein
Alexander I, Franz I, and Frederick William III of Prussia at the Peace of Paris, 1814

M. C. De Vries, Jr.
Representation of **The Night Watch**, Famous Painting by Rembrandt (reverse of Rembrandt medallion)

half a century, was a death commemorative struck in 1879 honoring the poet Joost van den Vondel. Another death commemorative, done in 1876, represents the sole medal of Jewish content issued by de Vries, namely for Samuel Leonardus Verveer, the Dutch landscape and genre painter.

A lesser-known Dutch medalist was A. L. Snoek, born in 1840 and also listed elsewhere as M. A. Snoek.[15] Snoek was the court engraver of the Queen Widow of Holland in Amsterdam and had already received notice at the age of eighteen. In 1863 he struck a Jubilee Medal on the Independence of Holland and in 1891 the Agricultural Prize Medal for the town of Waalwijk. He also produced folk medals and badges of local interest.

The third Dutch medalist, and perhaps the one with the most enduring reputation, was Jacques Elion. As was the case with many earlier Jewish engravers, his father paved the way. Samuel Cohen Elion (1815–1880) was a medalist and gem cutter in Amsterdam, known for his portrait cameos. The son, Jacques, who lived from 1842 to 1893, at first preferred graphic art, which he studied with his father and then at the Amsterdam Academy. Medals of reputation are: the 1866 Award to Volunteer Doctors during the Cholera Epidemic; the 1872 Third Centenary of Dutch Independence; the 1883 portrait of Gisb. von Tienhoven, mayor of Amsterdam; and two of special Jewish interest, the 1865 commemorative on the Opening of the New Building of the Amsterdam Jewish Boys' Orphanage and the 1879 Commemoration of Michael H. Godefroi for Thirty Years' Service in the States-General (the Dutch Congress). The Christian Huygens Gold Medal of the Dutch Society of Sciences, presented to Simon Newcomb in 1878 for merit in astronomy, is on exhibition at the Museum of History and Technology, Smithsonian Institution, Washington, D.C.

Only one 19th-century Bohemian Jewish medalist is known.[16] He was Jakob B. Resek, born in 1805 at Pless. Resek, who had an even greater reputation as a portrait gem engraver, received the Prussian gold medal

Jacques Elion
Opening of Hebrew Orphan Asylum, Amsterdam, 1865

of art in 1844 from King Frederick William IV for his work with gems. We have on record four of his medals: a commemorative struck for the 1848 New Austrian Constitution; an undated portrait medal of the concert singer Jenny Lutzer; and two of Jewish interest – an 1845 death memorial portrait for Simon Edler von Laemel, the Bohemian merchant for whom the first Jewish secondary school in Jerusalem (1856) was named, and an 1847 portrait of the composer Meyerbeer, done in the last year of Resek's life.

An isolated Polish piece – unique in view of that country's tortured Jewish population – is the 1843 First Jewish Confirmation for Girls at Warsaw. This was done by Eichel, a miniature painter and gem engraver of whom we know little except that he executed a few medals.[17]

English Jewry during the 19th century produced two figures who may be included in this study, though the men were not technically medalists.[18] The first, Hyam Hyams, commissioned and distributed medals in the early part of Queen Victoria's reign. In 1848 he issued a series of model crowns cut by Allen and Moore of Birmingham, some of which bear the initials "A & M," while others are engraved "Pub. by H. Hyams." Of more significance, Hyams commissioned two Jewish medals of excellent caliber, an 1836 death memorial for Nathan Mayer Rothschild and a portrait commemorative in 1843 for Solomon Hirschel, Chief Rabbi for the Ashkenazi community of England. Collectors of Jewish medals place both of these high on their list of valued medals.

A similar figure appeared forty years later in the person of A. D. Loewenstark, who organized his die-sinking firm of A. D. Loewenstark & Sons with two branches in London. The business venture failed, and in 1895 Loewenstark emigrated to Rhodesia. This firm produced a number of prize medals, mainly of a sporting and masonic nature. Of interest to Jewish collectors is a Centenary Commemorative for Sir Moses Montefiore in 1884.

Jakob B. Resek
Death Memorial for Simon Edler von Laemel, 1845 (obverse)

Eichel
First Jewish Confirmation for Girls at Warsaw, 1843

Hyam Hyams

Solomon Hirschel, Chief Rabbi for Ashkenazi Community of England
(obverse)

Death Memorial for Nathan Mayer Rothschild, 1836
(obverse)

A. D. Loewenstark (obverse)
Centenary Commemorative for Sir Moses Montefiore, 1884

The United States first enters the lists in the very early 19th century[19] with a medalist of fine reputation in his time. He was Moritz Furst (1782–1840), born near Pressburg, Hungary (now Bratislava, Czechoslovakia), and educated in Vienna. Furst for a time did die cutting for the Royal Mint of Lombardy but came to America in 1807 with the encouragement of the American Consul in Leghorn. He worked as an engraver (though not with official status) for the U.S. mint in Philadelphia from 1812 to 1839, returning to Europe shortly before his death.

Furst received quick recognition and was commissioned over and over to do patriotic portraits and commemoratives. Among his most striking medals of the War of 1812 are Captain Oliver H. Perry and the Capture of the British Fleet on Lake Erie, Major Gen. Winfield Scott for Chippewa and Niagara, Major Gen. William Henry Harrison for the Battle of The Thames, and Major Gen. Andrew Jackson and the Battle of New-Orleans. The original gold strike of this last medal is in the collection of the American Numismatic Society in New York City. By order of Congress, Furst did portrait medals of presidents James Monroe, John Quincy Adams, Andrew Jackson, and Martin Van Buren.[20] Other medals executed for commissions outside the mint include portraits of William Penn, George Washington, Alexander Hamilton, James Madison, Dr. Benjamin Rush, and New York Governor De Witt Clinton. Moritz Furst also has to his credit the first recorded American Jew-

Moritz Furst

Governor Isaac Shelby of Kentucky, with General Harrison, at the Battle of the Thames, October 5, 1813

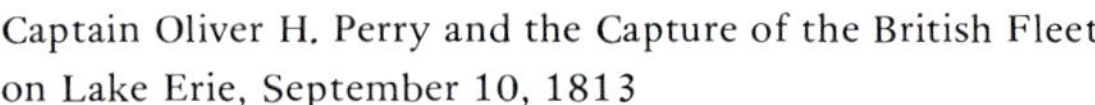

Captain Oliver H. Perry and the Capture of the British Fleet on Lake Erie, September 10, 1813

Moritz Furst

Major General Andrew Jackson Beats the British at New-Orleans, War of 1812

Death Memorial for Gershom Mendes Seixas, 1816

ish medal, the excessively rare homage on the death in 1816 of Gershom Mendes Seixas, the patriot rabbi during the American Revolution and lifelong trustee of Columbia College.

Much later, another American drew acclaim in this field, though his medals are secondary to his sculpture. This was Isidore Konti, who was born in Vienna in 1862 and emigrated to America in 1891. Konti, who first worked his trade in Chicago and then moved to New York City, became vice-president of the National Sculpture Society, and his work is represented at such museums as the Metropolitan Museum of New York. He designed the medal of the National Academy of Design and also did folk pieces. Of special Jewish interest is his 1905 medal commemorating the 250th Anniversary of Jewish Settlement in the United States.

Isidore Konti
250th Anniversary of Jewish Settlement in the United States, 1905

Jewish Medalists of the 20th Century

The 20th century is still not over, but already the number of Jewish medalists has been exceptional. For the sake of convenience, they may be divided into five categories and then classified within these categories according to nationality.[21] The first such category would be the major figures operating primarily as medalists: the American, Victor D. Brenner; the German, Benno Elkan; the Dane, Harald Salomon; and the Hungarians, Paul Vincze (who has lived in England for many years), Ede Telcs, and Fülop O. Beck. The second category would be famous sculptors who occasionally turn to medals, often with indifferent results — Americans such as William Zorach, Jacques Lipchitz, and Leonard Baskin and Germans like Hugo Kaufmann and Arnold Zadikow. The third category would be medalists of lesser fame, amounting to some two dozen. A fourth category would be medalists who, either through personal compulsion or due to a pattern of commissions, devoted themselves almost exclusively to medals of specific Jewish content. And the last category, whose importance will obviously increase in time, consists of Israeli medalists, though up to the present time certain of the best medals (both government and private) flowing from Israel have been engraved by nationals of other countries.

Americans can be proud of Victor D. Brenner (1871–1924), whose popular reputation rests on the fact that in 1909 he engraved the head on the Lincoln cent. This design is so pleasing that it has remained unchanged for over fifty years,[22] which makes it almost unique among American coins. But Brenner was an excellent medalist as well; in fact, the card file in the Metropolitan Museum of Art listing the various medals of this master is over two and a half inches thick. Born in Russian Lithuania, Brenner (born Barnauskas), whose father was a seal engraver, came to the United States at the age of nineteen and worked as a die cutter and engraver of badges. He then went to Paris for three years, where he studied under the great medalists Roty and Charpentier, returning to America as a mature artist. In a short time he became known as a master at combining high and low relief on portraits. It would be impossible to review the many medals of Brenner, but among his best portraits are those of Carl Schurz, James McNeill Whistler, Amerigo Vespucci, Adolph Werner (Professor at City College), John Paul Jones, the lawyer and statesman William Maxwell Evarts, and the railroad builder Collis Potter Huntington. Victor D. Brenner also engraved such commemoratives as the 1902 Visit of Henry of Prussia, the 1903 Lloyd McKim Garrison award for Harvard, the 1904 Centennial of the New York Historical Society, the 1906 Tallmadge award for the Sons of the American Revolution, the 1909 Centennial of Lincoln's Birth, the 1909 "Maternity," and the 1910 Hispanic Society of America Sorolla medal. The Charles P. Daly Gold Medal, presented in 1902 by the American Geographic Society of New York, is on exhibition at the Museum of History and Technology, Smithsonian Institution, Washington, D.C. Portraits of specific interest to collectors of Jewish medals include those of Rafael Joseffy, the pianist and composer; Solomon Schechter, an early president of the Jewish Theological Seminary of America; Mrs.

Victor D. Brenner
Prince Henry of Prussia Visits the United States, 1902

Victor D. Brenner

Carl Schurz

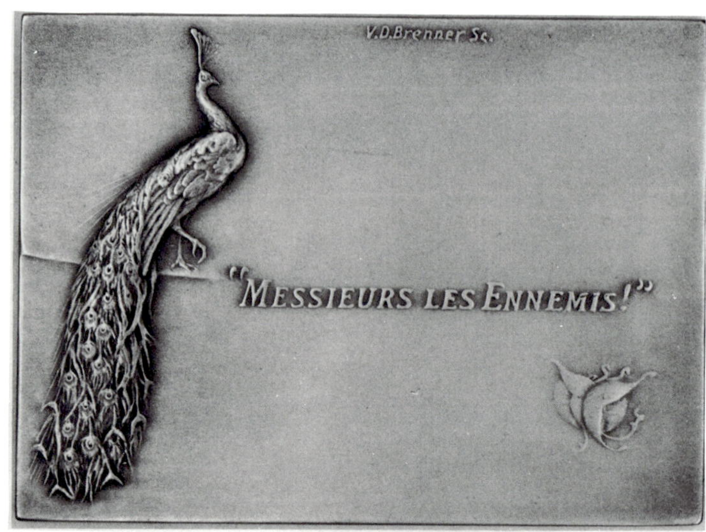

James McNeill Whistler

The Lincoln Cent, 1909 to Present

Julia W. Oettinger, the wife of his benefactor; Abraham Walkowitz, the painter; Jacob Schiff, the financier; and Solomon Loeb, founder of Kuhn Loeb & Co. Brenner is one of the very few holders of the J. Sanford Saltus Award of the American Numismatic Society, the highest U.S. award for proficiency in the art of the medal.

The German equivalent of Victor D. Brenner is Benno Elkan (1877–1960). Although he was born in Dortmund, he fled from Hitler in 1933 and resided in England for the rest of his life. Elkan was also a top sculptor, specializing in pieces of monumental size, most of which were destroyed by the Nazis. He has among his significant works two large Biblical candelabra in Westminster Abbey, a statue of Sir Walter Raleigh in Commerce Street, London, and a war memorial re-erected in the center of Frankfort on Main after World War II. But his masterpiece is considered the bronze Menorah; a gift from England, it now stands in front of the Parliament of Israel. Although artists are not often able to excel in two areas simultaneously, Benno Elkan was just as great a medalist as a sculptor, and at an early age he became a leader in the German revival of plaquettes and medallions. His specialty was portraiture, in which he is considered one of the great 20th-century masters. For this reason, Elkan was an artist much in demand in Germany during the pre-Hitler period and was commissioned to do pieces of many celebrities, especially in the field of commerce. Since the renown of these people was usually local, quite a few of them are now forgotten, but special mention might be made of Field Marshal von Mackensen, President Friedrich Ebert, the painter Hans Thoma, H.R.H. the Grand Duke of Baden, Geh. Rat. Dr. G. Wendt, and the architects Friedrich Ratzel and Carl Schaefer. Benno Elkan was proud of his Jewish lineage and modeled several of his German coreligionists. Perhaps his most famous medal is the memorial to Lieutenant Ludwig Frank, member of the Reichstag, who volunteered for war service and was killed in 1914. Among others of Jewish interest are portraits of the engineer Moritz Grunthal, the banker Louis Hagen, the merchant Alfred Tietz, the dermatologist Prof. Karl Herxheimer, the pianist Hedwig Einstein, and Foreign Minister Walter Rathenau. A very expressive piece is the portrait of the composer Gustav Mahler. After going to England, Elkan continued in this line, and to this later period we owe portraits of Joseph Hertz, Chief Rabbi of the British Empire; Lord Hugo Hirst of Witton; James Rothschild; and Claude Montefiore.

Denmark is the home of one of the great 20th-century Jewish medalists, Harald Salomon, whose work still upholds the classical principles of clarity and simplicity. In 1900 Harald Salomon was born in Oslo (then Christiania), Norway. Brought by his parents to Denmark in 1914, he studied to be a sculptor at the Danish Royal Academy of Beaux-Arts from 1922 to 1927. Salomon started to work for the Royal Mint in 1925, while at school, and became its head in 1933, retiring in 1968 after 43 years of service. Since 1930 he has executed all Danish money as well as state medals. Both his sculpture and medals are exhibited in many museums, especially in the Nordic countries. Four of his medals are on exhibition at the Smithsonian Institute's Museum of History and Technology in Washington, D.C.

The fruit of this labor over thirty years – amounting to over one hundred medals – can only be touched on, especially as the greater part was devoted to Danish personalities, notable in their own country but not a part of the world stage. Among the better-known persons done by Harald Salomon are Sir Winston Churchill, Hans Christian Andersen (a magnificent portrayal), Professor Willy Munck, King Constantine of Greece, and King Gustave VI of Sweden; his many portraits of the rulers of Denmark are naturally to be seen on both coins and medals. Of Jewish interest are the 70th Anniversary portrait of Professor Niels Bohr, the world-famous atomic scientist, whose mother was from a prominent Jewish banking family of Denmark; a cast plaque of Efrem Kurtz, the musical conductor; and a similar cast of David Ben-Gurion.

Probably the best-known Jewish medalist of our time

Benno Elkan
Lieutenant Ludwig Frank
(member of Reichstag, killed in World War I, 1914)

Benno Elkan
Walter Rathenau, Foreign Minister of Germany

Harald Salomon
70th Birthday of Niels Bohr

Harald Salomon

Hans Christian Andersen

King Frederick IX and Princess Anne-Marie of Denmark, 1964
5 Kroner

Christian X University Award

is Paul Vincze, born with the name Weiss to a religious family in Hungary in 1907. Vincze won a scholarship to Rome in 1935, where he studied for two years. He then settled in England and rapidly earned an esteemed reputation for a classical gift of portraiture balanced by allegorical reverses. This style has also been expressed in coins, and Vincze has designed some of the national currency for nations such as Ghana, Libya, Nigeria, Malawi, Guinea, Guatemala, and Paraguay. The portrait of Kwame Nkrumah of Ghana on the ten-shilling coin of 1958 and that of Sir Alexander Bustamente on the Jamaican dollar of 1967 are especially pleasing.

The medals of Paul Vincze are legion and have been exhibited in the top institutions of the Western world, including the British Museum, U.S. Smithsonian Institution, and the Bibliothèque nationale in Paris. The American Numismatic Society in New York City has a permanent display of his large cast medallions. Vincze also received the first Gold Medal of the American Numismatic Association, issued in 1966, as the outstanding medalist of the year. Some of his most significant portrait commemoratives are: the 1953 Coronation of Queen Elizabeth II at Westminster, the 1955 150th Anniversary of the Battle of Trafalgar, the 1957 Dedication of the Harry S. Truman Library, the 1957 Independence of Ghana, the 1964 400th Anniversary of William Shakespeare, the 1965 Award Medal for the Smithsonian Institution, the 1966 50th Anniversary of the Irish Revolution, and the 1970 Charles Dickens Death Centennial. Portrait medals best known are those of President and Mrs. Truman, Sir Winston Churchill, Arturo Toscanini, Earl Attlee, Lord Beveridge, the Aga Khan, and Marconi. His set of twelve zodiac medals is also well known.

Vincze, like Benno Elkan, has done quite a few medals of Jewish interest. In fact, some of the finest commemoratives of our time dealing with this subject come from his studio. Special mention might be made of the 1959 Interior of the Spanish and Portuguese Synagogue in London and the 1956 300th Anniversary of the Re-

Harald Salomon
Efrem Kurtz

Paul Vincze

Coronation of Queen Elizabeth II of Great Britain, 1953
(obverse)

President Harry S. Truman
(obverse)

300th Anniversary of the Resettlement of the Jews in Great Britain, 1956

Paul Vincze

Yehudi Menuhin at 50
(obverse)

Commemorative of the Reopening of the Jewish Museum in London; Interior of the Bevis Marks Synagogue
(reverse)

For the Late John Walker, Keeper of Coins and Medals, British Museum

Ede Telcs

Count G. Y. Andrassy

settlement of Jews in Great Britain. He has executed half a dozen medals issued by Isnumat, a private mint in Israel; perhaps the leading two of this group are the John F. Kennedy Memorial and the Visit of Pope Paul VI to the Holy Land. Vincze has been employed by the government of Israel as well and is responsible for the 1966 eulogy to Edmond and James de Rothschild and the 1967 Jubilee of the Balfour Declaration. Also to be noted are several portraits of Jews, including those of Viscount Herbert Samuel, Ben-Gurion, Lord Nathan, Emanuel Shinwell, and Yehudi Menuhin.

There are two other very distinguished and somewhat earlier Hungarian medalists. Ede Telcs (1872–1958), a convert to Christianity, studied at the Viennese Academy of Art. He received many international prizes for his medals, and his studio was the center of training for most of the contemporary Hungarian medalists, including Paul Vincze. During World War I, Telcs became the official war medalist for Hungary and did portrait pieces of the top military leaders, the best known being General de Falkenhayn. His most signifi-

Adolf Sonnenthal

Fűlop (Philip) O. Beck

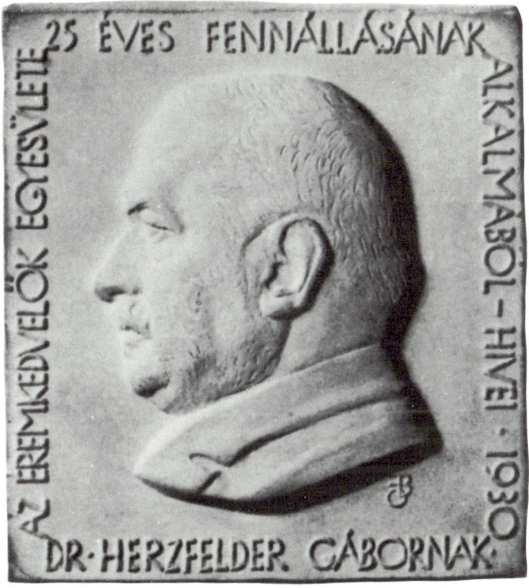

Dr. Gabor Herzfelder, 1930

Allegoric Reverse for Portrait of Paul Merse on His 70th Birthday, 1915

cant medals are: Count G. Y. Andrassy, Prime Minister of Hungary; the composer Giaccomo Puccini; A. Gorgey, a leader of the 1848 Hungarian Revolution; and Queen Wilhelmine of Holland. Telcs was so outstanding that, despite his Jewish origin, he was commissioned to portray Admiral Horthy, the Hungarian Fascist regent.

Telcs also did many medallic portraits of outstanding Austro-Hungarian Jews. He personally presented five plaquettes to the Budapest Jewish Museum, which thus might be considered the most important according to his own judgment. They represent Armin Wertheim and his wife; Professor Adam Politzer, the Hungarian otologist; Adolf Sonnenthal, the Austrian actor; Arnold Loewenstein; and a dual piece of Ignac Alpar and Baron Zsigmond Kornfeld. Other portraits of this type include the journalists Mikfa Falk and Ignac Fekete, the banker Moriz Reismann, the historian H. Marczali, the neurologist Moriz Benedikt, and the cellist David Popper. The Budapest Jewish Museum has a half dozen others of lesser-known persons. Telcs also did a self-portrait in 1931.

The records indicate that the highly gifted Hungarian Fűlop (Philip) O. Beck was also a baptized Jew.[23] Born in 1873 at Papa, he studied at the Fine Arts School of Budapest and later at the Ecole des Beaux-Arts in Paris. In 1896 he won a competitive prize for the medal of the Milliner's Exhibition, which launched his career. Beck did scores of medals dealing with Hungarian events and personalities. Three significant pieces on permanent exhibit at the American Numismatic Society in New York City are the Medal for Distinguished Visitors to Budapest; Dr. Istvan Toth, From his Pupils; and the portrait of Sir Aurel Stein, the Hungarian-born archaeologist who spent his creative years in the Far East. This last medal is of interest to Jewish collectors.

Beck's great reputation goes back to his young manhood: when the Hungarian Society of Friends of the Medal was asked to show a very small group of medals at the Brussels Salon de la Médaille in 1910, two of Beck's portrait pieces were chosen, those of Petofi,

Fulop (Philip) O. Beck

Medal for Distinguished Visitors to Budapest

Sir Aurel Stein

Andras Beck
Arnold Schoenberg
(obverse)

the Hungarian poet, and Mikes Kellmen, the Hungarian writer. The Budapest Jewish Museum also has in its collection almost a dozen plaquettes of other individuals.

It may be mentioned that Andras Beck, son of Fülop O. Beck, is likewise a distinguished sculptor and medalist. Born at Alsogod, Hungary, in 1911, he went to the Budapest Fine Arts School and stayed on as a professor. He later emigrated to Paris, where he is now much favored by the French Medal Mint. His two best-known early medals are portraits of the aesthete Schopflin and the writer Miklos Radnoti. Recent portrait pieces include the writer Thomas Mann; four musicians, Bela Bartok, Zoltán Kodály, Moussorgsky, and Arnold Schoenberg (the last of interest to collectors of Jewish medals); the plaque of the poet Saint John Perse; and the plaque of the sculptor Ossip Zadkine, likewise of Jewish interest.[24] Andras Beck's recent works are among the most avant-garde in the world, often dissolving the letters and figures in an abstract design.

Hugo Kaufmann
Max Liebermann

Occasional Medalists

A second category of 20th-century medalists is made up of the important Jewish sculptors who have only occasionally been commissioned to do medals. The earliest of these men, most of them German and born in the latter half of the 19th century, still considered the medallic art on a par with sculpture. Their work shows an accordingly high standard. The first is Hugo Kaufmann, who was born at Hesse in 1868 and died at Munich in 1919. Kaufmann was known mainly as a sculptor, and his monuments and outdoor fountains (a specialty of the artist) were scattered throughout Germany. Of a score of medallic works by Kaufmann, the best known are the 1897 portrait medal of Arnold Boecklin, the 1899 150th Goethe Anniversary commemorative, the 1903 plaquette on the 25th Anniversary of the Hoch Conservatorium, and the 1903 Prince Louis Medal of the Munich Geographical Society. Of Jewish interest, he also did a superior portrait medal

Arnold Zadikow
Self-Portrait

William Zorach
Pepsi-Cola Achievement Award
(reverse)

Jacques Lipchitz
Presidential Scholars Award
(reverse)

of Max Liebermann, the leader of the German impressionist school of painting.

A similar figure, though important more as a graphic artist than as a sculptor, was Emile Orlik. A product of an assimilated family, Orlik (1870–1932) was born in Prague and went to Berlin in 1905, where he became a professor of art. Known primarily for his graphic portraits of many of his distinguished contemporaries, Orlik designed a number of medals executed by the Berlin mint, as well as plaquettes.

Better known is the German Arnold Zadikow (1884–1943), who was born in the Baltic Sea town of Kolberg and killed by the Nazis at the concentration camp of Theresienstadt. Living mainly in Munich, Rome, and Paris, Zadikow specialized in sculpturing small objects, including terra cotta, glass, and silver figures. He also executed fine plaques and medals, among which perhaps the most prominent is his 1916 medal of Prince Regent Leopold, Regiment Bavarian Field Artillery. Arnold Zadikow also expressed interest in Jewish subjects: he engraved several medals of local notables, such as Meta Gutmann of Munich and the German collector Adolph Herz, as well as the 1913 50th Anniversary Jubilee at Kolberg of Rabbi Solomon Goldschmidt and the 1922 25th Anniversary of the B'nai B'rith Lodge of Munich.

Partly because of the exodus from Europe due to the Nazi terror and partly because America has come of age in the world of art, a significant number of Americans are represented in this category. The earliest is Joe Davidson (1883–1952), whose sculptured busts are world famous. Davidson also did occasional medals; a typical example is the 1942 portrait memorial to Pilot Officer Guy Levy-Despas, Royal Canadian Air Force, who was shot down at the age of twenty.

William Zorach (1887–1966) was born in Lithuania but spent almost his entire life in the United States. Zorach was one of the greatest masters of the technique of working directly with stone and wood, and his sculpture is in more than 80 museums and public buildings.

Leonard Baskin

The Smith College Award

The National Medal for Literature Award (obverse)

Like Davidson, Zorach did occasional medals. Three examples are the Dimitri Mitropoulos International Music Competition Award, the Pepsi-Cola Achievement Award, and the *Look* Magazine Achievement Award.

Chaim Jacob (Jacques) Lipchitz (1891–1973), born in Lithuania, is too well known as a sculptor to need comment. An important member of the School of Paris, he came to New York City in 1941 and stayed in this country. An example of the medallic art of Lipchitz is the Presidential Scholars Award, with a portrait of President Johnson. Lipchitz also did a very unusual medal for The Jerusalem Foundation that has a primeval crudeness.

Two somewhat younger Americans complete this list of incidental medalists. They are Chaim Gross and Leonard Baskin. Gross recently did a large portrait plaque of stylized grandeur, called the Herbert Lehman Israel Award. Baskin, who seems to be trying out the field of medals, has struck several pieces in the last few years, the Smith College Award, the National Gallery of Art Award, the National Medal for Literature Award, and a portrait commemorative for the painter Thomas

Leo Horovitz
Centenary of the Frankfort Philanthropin, 1904

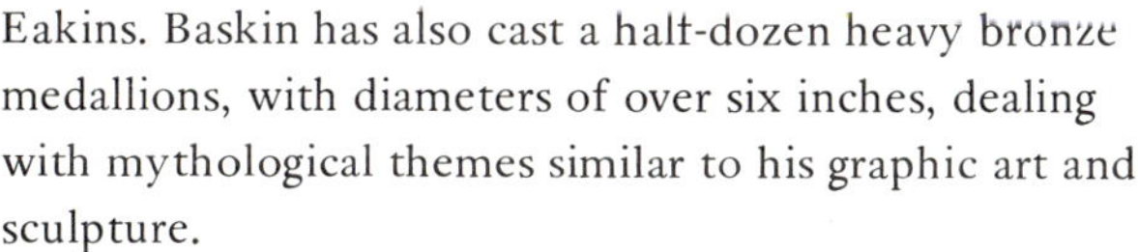
Eakins. Baskin has also cast a half-dozen heavy bronze medallions, with diameters of over six inches, dealing with mythological themes similar to his graphic art and sculpture.

Lesser-Known Modern Medalists

A third category, 20th-century Jewish medalists of decent but not spectacular reputation, runs into the dozens. These men can only be touched on, for a review of their individual works would be too lengthy.

Three Germans lived in the transitional period between the old and new centuries. The earliest was Leo Horovitz, sometimes spelled Horowitz (1876–c.1960), who was the son of a very well-known rabbi in Frankfort on Main and (like Joel, son of Rabbi Lippman Levi in Holland almost two centuries before) engraved mainly Jewish medals. His best-known work is the 1904 Centenary of the Frankfort Philanthropin, one of the first Jewish high schools in Germany. Portrait medals or plaquettes include those of his father, Marcus Horovitz, his brother, Dr. Joseph Horowitz, the painter Armin Stern, the philanthropist Louis Feist, the banker Charles Hallgarten, and the philosopher Hermann Cohen, to mention the more prominent persons. Second is Max Lewy, whose most distinguished medals are those of J. Schottlander, the German grain merchant, and the 1917 portrait of the German banker Alexander Fiorino. And the third, a woman, is Else Fuerst, later killed by the Nazis, who is known for her portraits of Max Buechlein, R. von Woldeck, and Henriette Goldschmidt, the leader of the German suffragette movement. With the exceptions of Buchlein and Woldeck, all these medals are of interest to the Jewish collector.

Only one such Jewish medalist appears in Austria,[25] but he has a fine reputation. This is Arthur Loewental, who was born at Vienna in 1879 and died in London around 1966. Loewental was also a sculptor and gem engraver. He initiated a series of portrait medals as a very young man, patronized by the Vienna Jewish community. These include Moriz Kanitz, 1898; Salo Cohn, 1901; Adolf Hoffmann, 1902; and Wilhelm Lichtenstern, 1904. During World War I he did a series of commemorative pieces, covering both military persons and events, several being of great suggestive power. Two

Leo Horovitz
Rabbi Marcus Horovitz

later plaques, of Albert Einstein and Rufus Daniel Isaacs, First Marquess of Reading, show his fine grasp of the classical style, as does a 1965 memorial medal for Winston Churchill. Loewental's portrait of Rudyard Kipling is on permanent exhibit at the American Numismatic Society in New York City. It is the personal conviction of the writer that, unlike that of many artists of our epoch, the artistic stature of Arthur Loewental will grow rather than diminish with time.

Four medalists from Holland require inclusion, namely, Abraham Roth, Louise Metz, Ruth Brouwer, and A. A. Moorlag. Two medals of "Bram" Roth were exhibited at the Paris International Exposition of Contemporary Medalists, held in 1957: Youth Plays and the Foundation of the Academy of Physical Culture at La Haye. Louise Metz, a distinguished sculptor as well, was born at Amsterdam in 1918. She is noted for a 1954 Dutch Literary Award and portraits of Van Gogh, Rubens, Erasmus, Breughel, Jefferson, Spinoza, Modigliani, and Sarah Bernhardt, the last three of Jewish interest. Her 1968 Opening of the New Building of the Netherlands Bank of Amsterdam received the high honor of being one of the few medals illustrated in the Catalogue of the 13th Congress of the International Federation of the Medal, held in 1969 at Prague. Certain of Louise Metz's work has been done for the French Medal Mint, where she specializes in sportive medals. Ruth (Ryth) Brouwer, born at Antwerp in 1930 and an expert in casting, has attained a considerable reputation. Among her best-known medals are the Commemoration of the 1945 Liberation (issued in 1960), the 1963 Two Young Girls of Surinam, the 1965 Centenary of the Vondelpark at Amsterdam, and the 1967 Three Magi. She has also done several folk Jewish castings, such as the 50th Anniversary of Tante Shellie and the Portrait of Saartje Blom. Albert Abraham Moorlag was born in 1928 of a Roman Catholic father and a Jewish mother. Persecuted by the Germans during World War II, he identified with his Jewish maternal background and, since graduating from the Royal Academy of Rotterdam, has done

Arthur Loewental
General Oberst von Kluck, The Drive on Paris, 1914–1915
(iron medal)

Arthur Loewental
Otto Weddigen, Commandant of U-Boat No. 29, World War I (iron medal; obverse)

medals almost exclusively of Dutch Jews or Israelis. His heavy cast bronze portraits, with their high relief and exaggerated features, verge on caricature. Perhaps most successful is his study of Chaim Weizmann.

Hungary produced some other medalists aside from those previously noted. The most prolific was István (Stephan) Csillag, born in 1881, among whose Hungarian Jewish portrait pieces can be included the painter Lajos Bruck, the publisher Zsigmond Falk, the oculist and medical writer Professor Vilmos Goldzieher, the former Director of the Budapest Jewish Museum, Fülop Gruenwald, and the famous Rabbi Simon Hevesi. Another half-dozen portraits could easily be cited. Csillag also did a rather large self-portrait plaque. Also to be noted is the medalist Jeno F. Kormendi, born in 1886 and a baptized Jew. His best-known Jewish studies include the insurance magnate Morris Ribarí, as well as Armin Vámbéri and Alfred Brull. A third Hungarian medalist is Aladar Gárdos, born in 1878, whose most popular medal is a portrait of the esteemed German rabbi, Meyer Kayserling. A fourth is Mark Vedres, born in 1870, responsible for the portrait of Ede Harkányi. Of course, these men turned out hundreds of medals,[26] but the examples have been deliberately chosen from the collection of the Budapest Jewish Museum for the convenience of Jewish collectors.

The Hungarian Jews dominated the medallic art of their country in the 19th and 20th centuries. Aside from the prominent figures like Moritz Furst, Paul Vincze, Philip Beck, and Ede Telcs, as well as the lesser known figures just discussed, the famous folio of Lajos Huszár and Béla Procopius, *Medaillen-und Plaketten-*

Arthur Loewental
Rufus Daniel Isaacs, First Marquess of Reading

Louise Metz

Thomas Jefferson

Amedeo Modigliani

Ruth (Ryth) Brouwer
Portrait of Saartje Blom

István (Stephan) Csillag
Dr. Simon Hevesi, Chief Rabbi of Budapest, 1925

Boris Bernstein
The Strike
(obverse)

kunst in Ungarn (Budapest, 1932) discusses many others with Jewish names. Putting aside those with names that may or may not be Jewish (such as Klein, Kiss, and Farkas), also listed are: David Adler, Ede Adler, Jakab Adler, Ernoe Adler, Arpad Basch, Jozsef Friedmann, and Frigyes Littmann.

The medallic art is upheld in 20th-century France and the United States largely by two organizations, namely, the arm of the French government called la Monnaie (the Medal Mint), with its subsidiary, le Club français de la Médaille, and the nonprofit Society of Medalists in America. Both sponsor medals, the former mainly to celebrate Gallic culture[27] and the latter to encourage and develop American artists. Each in its own way has changed what might have been an aesthetic desert into, if not a verdant forest, at least a flourishing garden.

France, despite its magnificent tradition of medal making, has brought forth few top Jewish medalists in our time. The earliest 20th-century figure is Emile August Marcus, Parisian born, and a gem engraver as well. At the 1902 Paris Salon he exhibited a medal of Saint George, and in 1903, one of the Aero-Club of France. In the same period Charles August Abram, born at Besançon, and presumed Jewish by name, exhibited four medals at the Paris Salon of 1905, as well as plaquettes in 1906 and 1907. Also to be included is Alexandre Zeitlin, Russian-born but a long-time resident of Paris. At the 1912 Paris Salon he exhibited two portrait medals of aristocrats and a plaquette of Flammarion, the French astronomer and author.

The first of the more contemporary French group, Boris Bernstein, was born at Lyons in 1907.[28] Among his better-known medals are portraits of Theodore Rousseau, Serge Lifar, and Martin Schongauer, and commemoratives for the French Union and UNESCO. Bernstein also specializes in allegoric medals, like his Architecture, Electronics, The Strike, and Our Force: To be United.

Born at Lvov, Poland, in the same year as Boris Bernstein was Léopold Kretz, who emigrated to Paris in 1931. Kretz, who managed to live in France clandestinely during the entire Nazi occupation, is a well-known sculptor who has executed monumental works as well as figures and busts. Of his large plaques cast in a free style, Meeting and Confluence may be mentioned; portraits are those of Georges Auric, Chaim Soutine, and Jules Pascin, the last two of Jewish interest.

André Bloc, born at Paris in 1908, is one of the most respected senior engravers of the French Mint, having worked there since 1937. He has done several medals, including a group of famous painters – Albrecht Durer, Franz Hals, and Caravaggio. Perhaps his most interesting medal is a portrait of Lenin[29] with a contrasting effect through the use of patina.

Simon Goldberg, also born at Paris in 1913, is a sculptor, painter, and book illustrator, as well as a medalist. Goldberg has done several portrait medals, including those of Corot, Bizet, and Daumier; a superior large cast medal in the romantic style is his Happy Family.

Abram Krol, born in 1919 of a Hassidic Polish family, came to France in 1938 and survived the Nazi period. Known as an engraver of high-quality book illustrations, he has recently started casting medals and plaques. Two works commissioned by the French Mint deal with Jewish subjects, namely, The Torah and The Sacrifice of Abraham.

Shelomo Selinger, born in 1928 in Poland, spent the years 1941 to 1945 in a concentration camp; he was released at the age of seventeen. An illegal immigrant to Palestine, he started to sculpt at a kibbutz. Winner of the Norman prize, he went to France to perfect his technique. Though mainly known as a sculptor in granite, Selinger has also done several medals, including The Couple, Samson and the Lion, Birth of Pegasus, and The Wise Women, after Molière's play of that name.

Among the Jewish medalists presently working in France, an exciting artist is Esther Gorbato, born 1931

Léopold Kretz
Chaim Soutine

André Bloc
Lenin

in Buenos Aires, Argentina. An extremely gifted sculptor and painter as well, Esther Gorbato studied at both the Ecole des Beaux-Arts and the Ecole des Arts Appliqués of Paris. She was then elected professor of Architectural Design at the Ecole des Beaux-Arts, the first woman ever made a professor. Among her more distinguished medals are portraits of the economist Charles Braibant, Nietzsche, Saint Teresa of Avila, Saint Thomas Aquinas, Roualt, and Camille Pissarro. The Nietzsche and Pissarro medals were exhibited at the Exposition Internationale de la Médaille held at Paris in 1967; and in the opinion of the writer, the Pissarro piece is among the finest portrait medals in all history of a Jew done by a Jewish medalist.

Besides Victor D. Brenner, there have been at least a dozen other American Jews actively engaged in the medallic art during this century. One of the earliest, the Austrian-born Emil Fuchs (1866–1939), is also among the best. Fuchs, as is apparent from his production, spent several years in England before coming to the United States. Mention may be made of the following medals: the 1900 Queen Victoria in the 63rd Year of Her Reign; the 1901 Coronation of King Edward VII with Queen Alexandra; the 1902 Triumphant End of the South African War; the 1906 Founding of the Hispanic Society of America; the 1908 50th Anniversary of the American Numismatic Society; the 1909 Hudson-Fulton Celebration; and portraits of John Pierpont Morgan, Robert Woolston Hunt, and H. J. Heinz. Of interest to the Jewish collector are several portrait medals of various members of the Rothschild family, which were done by Fuchs while he was living in Europe.

The last quarter of the 19th century gave birth to four other Americans, though not all were born in the United States. They were Frederick G. R. Roth, Louis Rosenthal, Leo Friedlander, and Bashka Paeff.

Frederick Roth (1872–1944) is noted for the medals of Distinguished Service to Education and the New Jersey State Teachers Association. The three best-known

Simon Goldberg
Happy Family
(obverse)

Esther Gorbato

Camille Pissarro

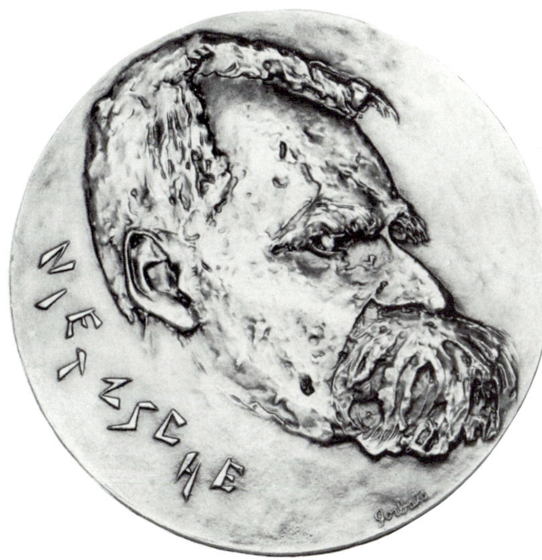

Friedrich Wilhelm Nietzsche

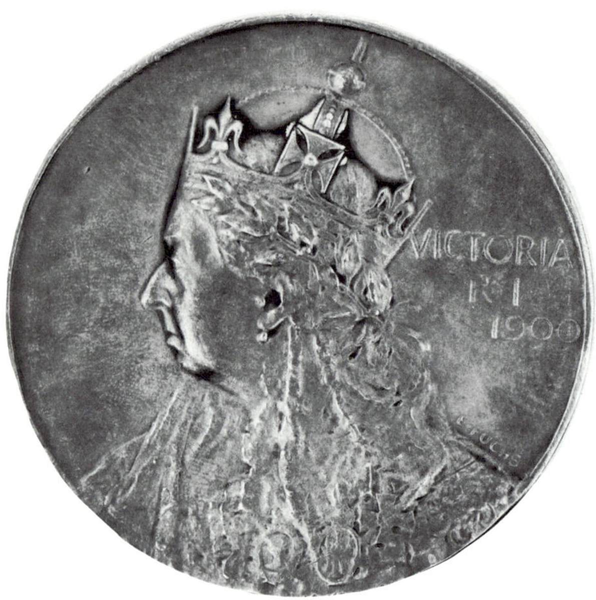

Emil Fuchs
Queen Victoria in the 63rd Year of Her Reign, 1900 (obverse)

Bashka Paeff
Dr. Simon Flexner

medals of Louis Rosenthal (1888–1964) – born Leon Chatel in Lithuania and an immigrant to the United States at nineteen – are the 1932 25th Anniversary of the Alpha Omega Fraternity, the 1938 Union of Faiths, and the 1938 Centenary of W. J. Dickey & Sons, owners of textile mills. Leo Friedlander (1890–1966), a sculptor as well, has been shown in exhibitions for his commission from the New York Building Congress and the 1949 Harmony, the 40th issue of The Society of Medalists. Perhaps the most distinguished among these four medalists is Bashka Paeff – born in 1893 in Minsk, Russia – whose statues of American personalities and war memorials are displayed at top U.S. institutions. The two noted medals of Bashka Paeff are those issued for the Boston University Alumni Association and the Rockefeller Institute, the latter being graced by a representation of Dr. Simon Flexner, head of the institute, and of interest to Jewish collectors.

The Medallic Art Company and the Franklin Mint, American firms operating for private profit, employ a group of contemporary artists in the medallic line that includes several of the Jewish faith. Perhaps the most prolific is Abram Belskie, born in London in 1907, whose work has been shown in international exhibitions. He has also received the very important J. Sanford Saltus Award. Belskie, who settled in the United States in 1929, is a specialist in medical and pharmaceutical medals, including the Lenox Hill Hospital Centennial, the New York Medical College, the American Medical Association, the Health Insurance Plan, the Endocrine Society, Johnson & Johnson, the American Optometric Association, the New York Obstetrical Society, the American Pharmaceutical Association, the College of Physicians and Surgeons, and the McNeil Laboratories. He has also done several medals for the New York University Hall of Fame, including those honoring the clergyman Phillips Brooks, the physician Walter Reed, and the dentist William Morton. Belskie struck The Goddess of Art in 1954, the 49th issue of the Society of Medalists. He was also commissioned to design the

Abram Belskie

Martin Luther King, Jr., Memorial Commemorative (obverse)

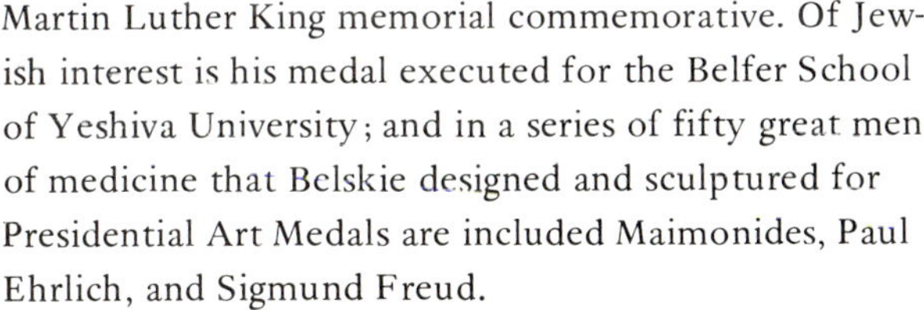

Martin Luther King memorial commemorative. Of Jewish interest is his medal executed for the Belfer School of Yeshiva University; and in a series of fifty great men of medicine that Belskie designed and sculptured for Presidential Art Medals are included Maimonides, Paul Ehrlich, and Sigmund Freud.

Born the year before, at New York City in 1906, was Adolph Block, whose medals include those for American Telephone and Telegraph, the Dictaphone Corporation, Tampa Drug Company, the American Chemical Society, the American Institute of Physics, the American Society of Human Genetics, and Georgetown University. Block struck The Pilgrim Landing in 1961, the 63rd issue of The Society of Medalists, as well as the medal celebrating Washington Irving for the New York University Hall of Fame.

Michael Lantz, born in 1908 at New Rochelle, New York, has executed medals for the *Saturday Evening Post,* Forbes, Inc., Kenneth H. Ripnen Co., an award medal for the City of New York, and two medals for the New York University Hall of Fame, those

The Goddess of Art

Adolph Block
Washington Irving

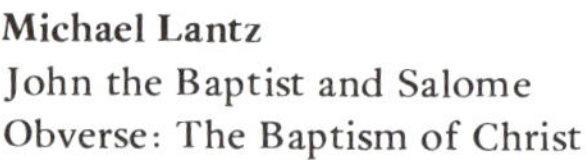

Michael Lantz
John the Baptist and Salome
Obverse: The Baptism of Christ

Reverse: Salome Holding Head of John

Albert W. Wein
God the Creator

celebrating Edgar Allan Poe and Oliver Wendell Holmes, Jr. Lantz also did John the Baptist and Salome in 1948, the 37th issue of the Society of Medalists.

Frank Eliscu, considered a sculptor more than a medalist, was born in New York City in 1912. With many works to his credit, he was elected president of the National Sculpture Society and served from 1967 to 1970. Two of his better-known medals are the Medal of Honor for the Architectural League of New York and the 70th issue of the Society of Medalists, Sea Treasures, issued in 1964. Eliscu was also picked in 1974 to design the reverse side of the official presidential inaugural medal of Gerald R. Ford.[30]

Albert W. Wein, born in 1915 in New York City, is responsible for the William Channing medal of the New York University Hall of Fame and, of Jewish interest, a recent portrait medal of Abba S. Eban, the former Israeli head delegate to the United Nations. Wein also was commissioned by the Society of Medalists and struck God the Creator in 1951 for its 43rd issue.

Four younger artists deserve mention here. Robert Berks has done two medals Jewish collectors might covet, the American Jewish Committee Herbert Lehman Human Relations medal and the 25th Anniversary of the Weizmann American Institute of Science. The former was one of seventeen American medals shown at the 1967 Paris International Exposition. Frederic V. Guinzburg was commissioned to do the Gold Medal of the Limited Editions Club and the Junior Red Cross Westchester County Chapter. Joseph Josephu did a meritorious award medal for the Metropolitan Police Department, one for Utah State University, and The Royal Family of Austria. Last to be mentioned is Nancy Dryfoos, who has executed two items of Jewish interest, the 1954 American Jewish Tercentenary and the Naomi Lehman Memorial Foundation Award.

Specialists in Jewish Medals

The 20th-century medalists noted, though Jewish, executed medals of Jewish interest only incidentally, in response to occasional commissions from Jews or Jewish organizations. But there is another category, Jewish medalists who concentrated on Jewish subjects to the exclusion of other material, the legitimate descendants of Joel of Amsterdam in the 18th century, Aaron Kohn in the 19th century, and Leo Horovitz in the very early 20th century. Most of these men, born in Europe and refugees from the Hitler terror, had developed under persecution a powerful sense of their Jewish background; through the medallic art they asserted pride in their ancestry. A good part of this production was commissioned by Samuel Friedenberg, the father of the writer, and is now on display or in the collection of the Jewish Museum of New York. The three principal medalists are Ivan Sors (Stern), Fred J. Kormis, and A. Eisenberg. To a somewhat lesser extent, Wera Mantel and Joseph Hovell also fit into this category. Their medals and plaques form a veritable encyclopedia in metal of world Jewry.[31]

The most prolific of these men was Ivan Sors (1895–c.1959). He was born in Hungary but worked in Prague as a cartoonist and illustrator up to the Hitler takeover, coming to the United States in 1940. Alone, his plaques are a gallery of Jewish genius, the portraits including such men as Isaac Abravanel, Leo Baeck, Simon Dubnow, Abraham and Simon Flexner, Heinrich Graetz, Moses Hess, Maimonides, Solomon Reinach, Judah P. Benjamin, Ernest Gruening, Vladimir Jabotinsky, Ferdinand Lassalle, Max Nordau, Leon Trotsky, Albert Ballin, Bernard Baruch, Otto Kahn, Adolph Lewisohn, Joseph Pulitzer, Felix Warburg, Fritz Haber, Bela Schick, Leon Bakst, Chaim Bialik, Edna Ferber, Lion Feuchtwanger, Hugo von Hofmannstahl, Joseph Israels, Emil Ludwig, Camille Pissarro, Jakob Wassermann, Max Weber, Franz Werfel, Stefan Zweig, Irving Berlin, Ernest Bloch, and Arnold Schoenberg.

Fred J. Kormis, born at Frankfort on Main in 1894, who has a fine reputation as a sculptor, also executed similar portrait plaques. He has lived in England since

Robert Berks
Herbert H. Lehman, American Jewish Committee Human Relations Award

1934, and many of his subjects belong to that nation. His best-known works are those of Judah Magnes, Manasseh ben Israel, Cecil Roth, Leslie Hore-Belisha, Harold Laski, Edwin Montagu, Israel Zangwill, First Viscount Samuel, and Georg Brandes, as well as Zionists like David Ben-Gurion, Itzhak Ben-Zvi, Moshe Sharett, and Chaim Weizmann.

The third medalist in this category is A. Eisenberg. His portrait plaques emphasize Americans and include Samuel Gompers, Sidney Hillman, Louis Brandeis, Nathan and Oscar Straus, Felix Frankfurter, Sir Jacob Epstein, David Belasco, Mischa Elman, George Gershwin, and Albert Einstein.

The remaining artists fitting into this category are Joseph Hovell and Wera Mantel. Hovell was born in Russia in 1897 and came to the United States around 1920. Mainly a sculptor, he is known for busts and bas-reliefs. His work includes medals of Herbert Lehman,

Ivan Sors
Felix M. Warburg

Ivan Sors
Rabbi Akiba Eger, the Younger

Fred J. Kormis
First Viscount Samuel (Herbert Louis Samuel)

Fred J. Kormis
Rabbi Judah Magnes

A. Eisenberg
George Gershwin

Joseph Hovell
Herbert H. Lehman
(approximately half size)

Wera Mantel
Rabbi Solomon Schechter

Wera Mantel
Cyrus Adler

Boris Schatz
Joseph Trumpeldor

Boris Schatz
Theodor Herzl Commemorative, 1904

Baron James de Rothschild, Jacques Halevy, and Jacques Offenbach. Wera Mantel modeled Rabbi Solomon Schechter, Louis Marshall, Mayer Sulzberger, Adolph Ochs, Berthold Auerbach, and Emma Lazarus.

Medalists of Israel

The last grouping of 20th-century medalists consists of Jewish nationalists operating in Palestine during the days of the British Mandate as well as those in present Israel. The earliest, and perhaps the most important, was Boris Schatz (1866–1932), born at Kovno in Latvia. Though named a professor at the Academy of Visual Arts at Sofia in 1895, Schatz heeded the Zionist call and settled at Jerusalem in 1906. There he founded the Bezalel School of Arts and Crafts and also organized the Bezalel Museum, now a part of Israel's National Museum. Schatz's dream – which had an important influence on the development of Israeli art in its early period – was to establish a national and folklorist Jewish art. A product of this outlook was some seventy plaquettes dealing with Jewish religious customs, orthodox Jewish types, and famous Zionist figures. Perhaps his best-known work is the Theodor Herzl death commemorative.

The creation of Israel as a separate state, with the autonomous right to strike coins and medals, has led to an indigenous class of artists. Though some foreign nationals are employed by the State mint – particularly Paul Vincze in England and André Lasserre in Switzerland[32] – Israelis are preferred. Miriam Karoli, born in Vienna in 1928, is prominent among them. Brought to Israel in 1939, she has designed many coins and medals for that government. Karoli is responsible for the reverses of the 1959 Ingathering of the Exiles, the 1960 Centenary of Theodor Herzl, and the 1962 10th Anniversary of the Death of Chaim Weizmann. She designed both sides of the 1958 10th Anniversary of Israel; the 1960 Hadassah Medical Center; a group of medals in 1962, including the World Council of Synagogues, the International Harp Contest, Music and Drama Festival,

André Lasserre and Miriam Karoli
Centenary of Theodor Herzl, 12th Anniversary, 1960
(reverse, by Lasserre) (obverse, by Karoli)

American Jewish Congress, and Shavit (that is, Comet) Launching; and two medals in 1963, the Israel Festival and Terra Sancta.

Another prominent figure is Zvi Narkiss, born in 1921 in Rumania. His medals are the 1958 Hanukkah commemorative, the 1959 Jubilee of Tel Aviv, the 1959 B'nai B'rith, the 1960 Bar Kokhba, the 1962 Negev Development, and the 1966 10th Anniversary of the Sinai Campaign. He also designed the reverse of the 1963 Seafaring commemorative.

Two brothers, Gabriel and Maxime Shamir, born in Latvia and brought to Israel in 1933, have achieved renown as designers. They are not only responsible for medals but have also designed the current Israeli bank notes, the Emblem of Israel, and many of that country's postage stamps. Their medals include the obverses of the 1961 Death of a Hasmonean Hero and the 1964 Chess Olympics. They designed both sides of the 1962 and 1963 Hanukkah commemoratives, the 1964 *Histadrut* or Labor Union Federation, the well-received 1964 Masada medal (with Nathan Karp), and the 1967 Jubilee of the Jewish Legion.

Another partnership is Rothschild and Lippmann, born in 1919 and 1920, respectively, and brought to Israel from Germany in their youth. Graduates of the Bezalel School, they often go under the amalgam of

Miriam Karoli
World Council of Synagogues, Jerusalem, 1962

Zvi Narkiss
Sinai Campaign, 1966

Rothschild and Lippmann
Tenth Anniversary of Israel, Medal of Honor, 1958

Rothschild and Lippmann
Third International Bible Contest, Jerusalem, 1964
(obverse)

Alex Berlyne and Jean David
Jaffa Coin-Medal
(reverse, by Berlyne)

(obverse, by David)

Alex Berlyne and Jean David
Jerusalem Coin-Medal
(reverse, by Berlyne)

(obverse, by David)

Jacob Zim
Twentieth Anniversary of Israel, Reunified Jerusalem, 1968

Selig Segal
Eighteenth Anniversary of Israel, 1966
"The People of Israel Live On"

Josef Bass
Third Pablo Casals International Violincello Competition, Jerusalem, 1961

Moshe Zipper
Twentieth Anniversary of the Warsaw Ghetto Uprising, 1963

Yitzhak Pugacz and Dodo Shenhav
Twentieth Anniversary of First Immigrant Blockade Runners, 1964
(obverse, by Pugacz)

(reverse, by Shenhav)

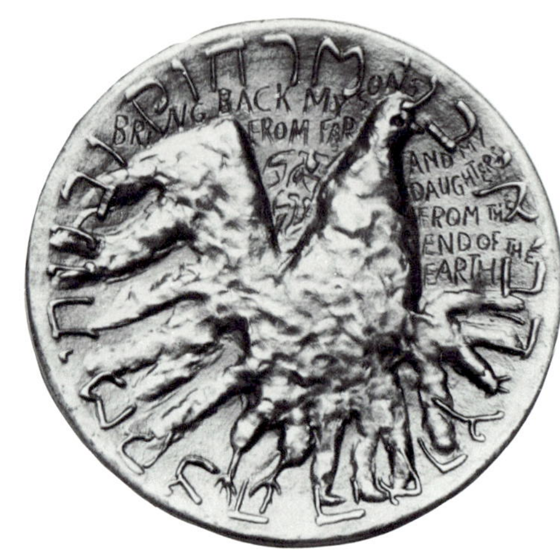

Ben Shahn (American)
Twentieth Anniversary of El Al

"Roli." Their medals include the obverses of the 1959 Ingathering of the Exiles, the 1963 25th Anniversary of Western Galilee Settlement, and the 1967 Port of Eilat, as well as the reverse of the 1960 Centenary of Henrietta Szold. They designed both sides of the 1958 and 1962 Medals of Liberation, the 1959 Medal of Valor, the 1960 Jubilee of Degania, the 1961 Bar Mitzvah of Israel, the 1961 and 1964 2nd and 3rd International Bible Competitions, and the 1967 Victory Commemorative.

A series of city medals issued by Israel, showing on one side an ancient coin of the site and on the other a modern representation of the same place, was issued mainly by two designers. Alex Berlyne, born in 1924, did those for Ashkelon and Lod, as well as the reverses for Acre, Tiberias, Beit She'an, Avdat, Caesarea, Jaffa, and Jerusalem. Mordechai Gumpel, born in 1912, did the obverses of Acre, Tiberias, Beit She'an, Avdat, and Caesarea. The remaining obverses, those for Jaffa and Jerusalem, were designed by Jean David. Both sides of the Jaffa and Caesarea city medals were honored by being illustrated in the Catalogue of the 13th Congress of the International Federation of the Medal, held in 1969 at Prague.

Mention should be made of Jacob Zim, born in Poland in 1922, who designed the obverse of the 1960 Centenary of Henrietta Szold, the reverse of the 1961 Death of a Hasmonean Hero, and both sides of the 1961 Kadman Numismatic Museum, the 1962 25th Anniversary of the United Jewish Appeal, the 1963 Zionist Organization of America, the 1964 10th Anniversary of the Bank of Israel, and the 1968 20th Independence Day commemorative. A similar figure is Josef Bass, born in 1914, who designed several medals in the early 1960s, including the Pentecostal World Convention, the 25th Anniversary of Benei Beraq, and the International Violoncello Competition. And the writer has found particularly powerful Moshe Zipper's 1963 medal commemorating the 20th Anniversary of the Warsaw Ghetto Uprising, also illustrated in the aforementioned catalog of the 1969 Congress at Prague. Other men who have participated in the design of Israel's medals are Yitzhak Behar, Selig Segal, Gabriel Neuman, Dodo Shenhav, Yitzhak Pugacz, Otto Wallish, Fred Pauker, and Barak Nachsholi.

The Jewish impact on world coinage, and particularly that of Europe, has been tremendous. The medieval coins referred to in Chapter I, whether issued under the aegis of viziers and potentates in Moslem countries or by mint masters or private lessees in Christian countries, were struck one thousand years after Emperor Hadrian's "final solution," when Judea was smashed to pieces, Jerusalem razed and the earth above its ruins freshly plowed to demonstrate, according to Roman custom, the death of the old and the inaugural of the new. And today, almost another thousand years later, not only are Jews still directing the mints and designing the coins for many countries, but the reborn state of Israel is again issuing money. After 70 C.E. the Emperors Vespasian and Titus struck a series of "Judaea Capta" – "Judea is Taken" – coins. The Israel government has issued medals with the slogan "Israel Liberata" – "Israel is Freed." But the Jewish people did not disappear in those two thousand years. And their footsteps in this long period are recorded in the coins and medals of the many nations where they lived and in which their influence is still felt.

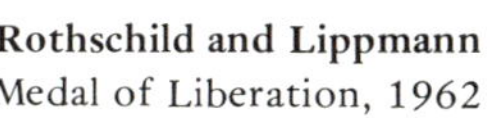
Rothschild and Lippmann
Medal of Liberation, 1962

Notes

Chapter I. Jewish Minters

1. D. M. Dunlop, **The History of the Jewish Khazars** (Princeton, N. J.: Princeton University Press, 1954), p. 227.

2. Ibid., p. 220.

3. Ibid., p. 231.

4. Daniel M. Friedenberg, "The Decline and Fall of the Falashas," **Judaism** (Summer 1956).

5. David Buxton, **Travels in Ethiopia** (London, 1951), p. 121.

6. H. Graetz, **History of the Jews,** Vol. III (Philadelphia, Pa.: The Jewish Publication Society of America, 1894), pp. 62–67.

7. Bruno Kisch, "Judaica in Nummis," **Historia Judaica,** Vol. 7 (1945), p. 143.

8. Albert Wolf, **Etwas über jüdische Kunst und ältere jüdische Künstler** (Hamburg, 1902), p. 24. Curiously, this information comes from an Arabic source five hundred years later (i.e., from around 1200), rather than from contemporary Jewish records. Cf. **Hebrew Union College Annual,** Vol. XVIII (1944), p. 290.

9. H. Graetz, **History of the Jews,** Vol. IV, p. 393.

10. S. D. Goitein, **A Mediterranean Society,** Vol. 1 (Berkeley and Los Angeles: University of California Press, 1967), pp. 362 and 365; also Vol. II (1971), pp. 106 and 544.

11. S. Asaf, **Searches and Sources** (Hebrew Society for Research and Excavation, 1960), pp. 197–199 (in Hebrew).

12. H. Graetz, **History of the Jews,** Vol. IV, pp. 393 and 395.

13. H. Graetz, **Geschichte der Juden,** Vol. X (1897), pp. 193 and 194. Also James Parkes, **A History of Palestine from 135 A.D. to Modern Times** (London: Victor Gollancz Ltd., 1949), p. 178.

14. Cecil Roth, **The House of Nasi: The Duke of Naxos** (Philadelphia, Pa.: The Jewish Publication Society of America, 1949), p. 200.

15. Ibid., p. 204.

16. Not included in this study are the many dozens of Christian medals, particularly from the 16th through 18th centuries, inscribed with the name of God in Hebrew letters. These attested merely to the revival of Hebrew learning in Protestant countries such as England, Holland, and Germany, and not to any Jewish interest or activity. This is also true for certain coins, such as those of Charles IX and Gustave II of Sweden and Christian IV of Denmark, likewise stamped in Hebrew.

17. Vicomte G. de Ponton d'Amecourt, "Description raisonée des Monnaies merovingiennes de Chalon-sur-Saône," **Annuaire de la Societé française de Numismatique et d'Archéologie,** Tome IV (Paris, 1873), pp. 128–131.

18. Juse of Mâcon (Civitas Matisconensium) sometimes signed Jusef. See Maurice Prou, **Les Monnaies Merovingiennes** (Paris, 1892), items 237–240. Jaco of Orléans (Civitas Aurelianorum) also signed Jacote: "Iacote Mo" – Belfort 503. Prou does not touch on Jewish moneyers in his exhaustive study other than stating there were "several of Hebraic origin," citing Jusef of Mâcon as an example. Belfort takes no position in the matter.

19. P. Bordeaux, "Les Ateliers monétaires de Toulouse et de Pamiers," **Revue Numismatique** (Paris, 1904), pp. 232–233. Given the name (a French derivation of Sasportas), the time, and place, it is the opinion of the late Cecil Roth and the writer that Louis de Saporta was of Jewish origin.

20. Louis Ciani, **Les Monnaies Royales françaises de Hughes Capet à Louis XVI** (Paris, 1926), p. 333. Also Jean Lafaurie and Pierre Prieur, **Les Monnaies des Rois de France,** Vol. II (Paris, 1956), pp. 133, 139, 141, 145, and 146. Also Adrien Blanchet, **Revue Numismatique,** 1910, pp. XXXVI–XXXVIII.

21. There are several cases of Jewish viziers in Moslem Spain, but these men operated as finance ministers, with administrative power over the mints, rather than mint masters. Their role will be discussed later.

22. G. C. Miles, "Bonnom de Barcelone," **Etudes d'Orientalisme dédiées à la mémoire de Lévi-Provençal** (Paris, 1962), pp. 683–693.

23. F. Cantera Burgos, "Christian Spain," Chap. XV in **The World History of the Jewish People,** ed. Cecil Roth, Vol. II (Tel-Aviv: Massadah Publishing Co., 1966), p. 378.

24. Yitzhak Baer, **A History of the Jews in Christian Spain,** Vol. I (Philadelphia, Pa.: The Jewish Publication Society of America, 1966), p. 146.

25. Ibid., Vol. II, p. 58.

26. Abraham A. Neuman, **The Jews in Spain,** Vol. II (Philadelphia, Pa.: The Jewish Publication Society of America, 1942), p. 237.

27. Yitzhak Baer, **A History of the Jews in Christian Spain,** Vol. II, p. 29.

28. Abraham A. Neuman, **The Jews in Spain,** Vol. II, p. 245.

29. Ibid., p. 252.

29a. Dr. Ya'akov Meshorer, Curator of Coins and Medals of the Israel Museum, has informed the author that he received for scrutiny a most curious lead token, shaped in the form and size of an English penny, from the British Museum. This object, found in an excavation at Wincester in a stratum from the 13th-century, has the obverse and reverse of a typical English coin of the time, except that the reverse has Hebrew lettering, indecipherable except for the end of a word which has the letters "ster", possibly referring to Wincester. This token, if genuine, would indicate that the Jewish community in 13th-century England issued community tokens, a revolutionary concept since there are no community tokens known among Jews from this time.

30. Joseph Jacobs, **The Jews of Angevin England** (London:

G. P. Putnam's Sons, 1893), pp. 392–396. The writer has excluded the names of Benedict, Davi, and Simon, because these would be quite common to Christians as well.

31. J. D. A. Thompson, **Inventory of British Coin Hoards A.D. 600–1500** (Oxford, England: Oxford University Press, 1956), Royal Numismatic Society.

32. Joseph Jacobs, **The Jews of Angevin England,** p. 73.

33. Cecil Roth, **A History of the Jews in England** (Oxford, 1949), pp. 12n and 115.

34. Cecil Roth, **The History of the Jews of Italy** (Philadelphia, Pa.: The Jewish Publication Society of America, 1946), p. 54.

35. V. Nahon, **Scritti in memoria di Sally Mayer** (Jerusalem, 1956), p. 368. Jaghel is also mentioned as a mint master in Correggio by Cecil Roth, **The Jews in the Renaissance** (New York: Harper & Row, 1965), p. 105.

36. Avv. Andrea Balletti, **Gli Ebrei e gli Estensi** (Reggio-Emilia, 1930), p. 163.

37. Max Grunwald, **History of Jews in Vienna** (Philadelphia, Pa.: The Jewish Publication Society of America, 1936), p. 3.

38. I.E. Scherer, **Die Rechtsverhaltnisse der Juden in den Deutsch-Oesterr Landen** (Leipzig: Duncker & Humblot, 1901), p. 121. Also Max Grunwald, **History of Jews in Vienna,** p. 2. Also **Germania Judaica,** Band 1, "Oesterreich," (Schlom), pp. 260, 261, 397, and 398. Also Julius Aronius, **Regesten zur Geschichte der Juden in Frankischen und Deutschen Reiche bis zum Jahre 1273** (Berlin: Leonhard Simon, 1902), No. 336, pp. 150 and 151; also No. 339, p. 152.

39. Max Grunwald, **History of the Jews in Vienna,** pp. 2 and 3.

40. Ibid., p. 6.

41. **Germania Judaica,** Band 1, pp. 32, 260, and 398. Also Julius Aronius, **Regesten,** No. 429, pp. 189 and 190; also No. 470, p. 206.

42. Max Grunwald, **History of Jews in Vienna,** p. 15.

43. Arnold Luschin von Ebengreuth, "Die Wiener Pfennige zu Zeiten Koenig Ottakars," Appendix, **Numismatische Zeitschrift,** XVI (Wien), p. 491.

44. Julius Cahn, "Ein Wetterauer Dynastenbrakteat mit hebraischer Umschrift," **Zeitschrift für Numismatik,** XXXIII (1923), p. 100. Also **Germania Judaica,** Band 1, "Allgemeines," p. 32.

45. Julius Cahn, "Unbekannte und seltene süd-und westdeutsche Mittelaltermünzen," **Frankfürter Münzzeitung,** No. 12 (December 1930), p. 178.

46. Julius Cahn, "Ein Wetterauer Dynastenbrakteat," p. 100. Also **Germania Judaica,** Band 1, "Meissen," pp. 225 and 226.

47. H. Buchenau, "Der Brakteatenfund von Seega," No. 313 (Marburg, 1905), p. 80. Also Bruno Kisch, "Judaica in Nummis," p. 146.

48. Moshe Boné, "Hebrew Inscriptions on Medieval Polish Official Coins," **Israel Numismatic Bulletin** (August–December 1962), p. 90. Also **Katalog Monumenta Judaica,** Sektion B, No. 172.

49. Julius Aronius, **Regesten,** No. 389, p. 173. Also **Germania Judaica,** Band 1, "Sachsen," p. 314.

50. **The Jewish Encyclopedia,** s.v. "Minters" (Funk and Wagnalls Co., 1907). Also Germania Judaica, Band 1, "Würzburg," (Jechial), p. 480. Also Julius Aronius, **Regesten,** No. 425, pp. 188 and 189. Also **Katalog Monumenta Judaica,** Sektion B, No. 171.

51. Marvin Lowenthal, **The Jews of Germany** (Philadelphia, Pa.: The Jewish Publication Society of America, 1936), p. 60.

52. **Encyclopaedia Judaica,** s.v. "Seals" (Jerusalem: Keter Publishing House Ltd., 1971), Vol. 14, p. 1080.

53. Münzen der Hohenstaufenzeit, Teil II, Nos. 1262 and 1263 (Auktion Hess-Leu am 8. und 9. März 1960 in Luzern), p. 192.

54. **Zeitschrift für Numismatik** (1887), p. 153. Also Eduard Fiala, **Ceske Denáry,** V. Praze (1896), pp. 63 and 64. Also **Numismatický Casopis Ceskoslovenský,** Vol. III (1927), Dr. Gustav Skalský, "O denárech vysehradský," pp. 186–188.

55. Julius Cahn, "Ein Wetterauer Dynastenbrakteat," p. 100.

56. **The Encyclopedia Britannica,** Fourteenth Edition, s.v. "Hungary," pp. 903 and 904.

57. Samuel Kohn, **A Zsidok Törtenete Magyarországon** (Budapest, 1884), pp. 50 and 51. Also Leopold Loew, **Graphische Requisiten und Erzeugnisse bei den Juden,** Vol. 1 (Leipzig, 1870–1871), p. 51.

58. Bálint Hóman, **Magyar Pénztörtenet (1000–1325)** (Budapest, 1916), pp. 462 to 468. It must be kept in mind that Hóman's material may be suspect, since he was a notorious anti-Semite.

59. Ladislaus Réthy and Gunther Probszt, **Corpus Nummorum Hungariae** (Graz, Chicago: Argonaut, Inc., 1967), pp. 71, 74, 77, and 89. Also Samuel Kohn, **A Zsidok,** pp. 100, 122, and 141.

60. **The Encyclopedia Britannica,** Fourteenth Edition, s.v. "Poland," p. 134.

61. Marian Gumowski, **Handbuch der Polnischen Numismatik** (Gratz, 1960). A fuller interpretation of this material appeared in an article by Moshe Boné, "Hebrew Inscriptions on Medieval Polish Official Coins," pp. 88–97.

62. The following historical account is an attempt to steer a middle course among different interpretations of what occurred during this troubled time of Polish history. All facts quoted are correct; I believe the interpretation is reasonable.

63. Excluded from this remark are two categories: coins issued by the Roman conquerors showing Jewish captives, and anti-Jewish coins from the European medieval period. As to the former, the first was issued in 54 B.C.E. by a lieutenant of

Pompey named Plautius. On the reverse is a kneeling figure with the legend "Bacchius Judaeus," interpreted by some historians, probably incorrectly, to represent the defeated Aristobulus. "Judaea Capta" coins, issued from Rome with Latin inscriptions and from Palestine with Greek inscriptions, depict Jewish captives after the First Revolt and consequent conquest. As to the second category, certain 12th-century bracteates show Jews stoning St. Stephen. The bracteates appeared in the bishopric of Halberstadt under Ulrich I (1149–1160). Julius Cahn, "Ein Wetterauer Dynastenbrakteat," also feels that a figure half-kneeling before a lord on a bracteate issued by David Hacohen in Wetterau represents a Jew bowing in fealty (this bracteate is illustrated on p. 12).

64. Ignace A. Polkowski, **Découverte à Glembokie des monnaies polonaises du moyen-âge** (Gnesen, 1876), p. 11.

65. Moshe Boné, "Hebrew Inscriptions," p. 95.

66. Ibid., p. 95.

67. Ibid., p. 95. According to **The Jewish Encyclopedia**, Abraham Esofowitz (or Jesofovich) converted and was elevated to the nobility; his brothers Michael and Isaac, however, remained Jews.

68. Israel Cohen, **History of Jews in Vilna** (Philadelphia, Pa.: The Jewish Publication Society of America, 1943), p. 4.

69. Ibid., p. 5.

70. Albert Wolf, **Etwas über jüdische Kunst**, p. 25. Also Koene, **Zeitschrift für Münz-, Siegel-und Wappenkunde**, Vol. V (1845), pp. 135–138.

71. L. Forrer, **Biographical Dictionary of Medallists** (London: Spink & Son Ltd., 1904–1912), alphabetic listing.

72. Several of Meir's coins are illustrated in The State Jewish Museum in Prague, **Prague Ghetto in the Renaissance Period** (Prague, 1965), pp. 22–25. See also Selma Stern, **The Court Jew** (Philadelphia, Pa.: The Jewish Publication Society of America, 1950), p. 218.

73. L. Forrer, **Biographical Dictionary of Medallists**, alphabetic listing.

74. Selma Stern, **The Court Jew**, p. 218. According to Bernhard Brilling, "Manasse von Hotzenplotz," **Jahrbuch der Gesellschaft für Geschichte der Juden in der Cechoslovakischen Republik** (Prag, 1935), Manasse was only the mint supplier in Silesia.

75. Peter Ujvary, ed., **Magyar Zsido Lexikon** (Budapest, 1929), p. 403. It might be added that shortly before this time an apostate by the name of János Ernuszt was the royal treasurer to King Matthias Corvinus of Hungary (1458–1490). It was not uncommon for Jews to convert in order to gain such posts and then continue to maintain intimate business relations, for mutual advantage, with their former coreligionists. See note 67 above.

76. Eduard Fiala, **Münzen und Medaillen der Welfischen Lande.** Teil: "Das mittlere Haus Braunschweig, linie zu Calenberg," (Wien, 1904), pp. 35 and 36.

77. J. Wilcke, **Christian IV's Møntpolitik i Aarene 1588–1625** (Copenhagen, 1919). Also Holger Hede, **Danmarks og Norges Mønter 1541–1814–1963** (Copenhagen, 1964). Information received from Julius Margolinsky, Librarian of the Jewish Community in Copenhagen.

78. Rabbi Dr. A. Ackermann, **Geschichte der Juden in Brandenburg on der Havel** (Berlin, 1906), pp. 58 and 60. Also Selma Stern, **The Court Jew**, p. 47. Also Emil Bahrfeldt, **Das Münzwesen der Mark Brandenburg (1415–1640)** (Berlin: Verlag von W. H. Kühl, 1895), pp. 219–232.

79. **Mitteilungen des Clubs der Münz-und Medaillenfreunde in Wien,** "Regesten aus J. Newald's Publication über Oesterreichische Münzprägungen," compiled by C. Oesterreicher, No. 8 (January 1891), p. 71.

80. Ibid., p. 81.

81. Selma Stern, **The Court Jew**, pp. 164 and 218.

82. J. -V. Kull, **Repertorium zur Münzkunde Bayerns**, Vol. II (München, 1903), p. 707.

83. L. Forrer, **Biographical Dictionary of Medallists,** alphabetic listing.

84. Glueckel of Hameln, **The Life of Glueckel of Hameln (1646-1724)** (New York: Thomas Yoseloff, 1963), pp. 171–174.

85. Franz Wolny, "Münzprägung der Fürstbischöfe von Olmütz in nichtprivilegierten Münzstatten," **Wiener Numismatische Zeitschrift** (1946), pp. 81 and 82.

86. Selma Stern, **The Court Jew**, pp. 162–176.

87. Heymann Jolowicz, **Geschichte der Juden in Königsberg** (Posen, 1867), p. 54. Albert Wolf, **Etwas über jüdische Künst** (p. 23), mentions Levin only as a mint.supplier.

88. Johannes J. Hartenstein, **Die Juden in der Geschichte Leipzigs** (Berlin, 1938), pp. 76–83. Also Selma Stern, **The Court Jew**, p. 211.

89. Selma Stern, **The Court Jew**, p. 164.

90. Simon Dubnow, **Welt Geschichte des Judischen Volkes von seinen Ur-Anfangen bis zur Gegenwart**, Band VII-des XVII und das XVIII Jahrhundert (Berlin, 1928), p. 309. A detailed account will be found in Selma Stern, **The Court Jew.**

91. Glueckel of Hameln, **The Life of Glueckel of Hameln (1646-1724)**, p. 85.

92. In 1758, the first year of the merger of the Itzig-Ephraim factions, the combination issued a rare debased 5-thaler piece, the gold content so low that the coin seems made of copper. Showing King Augustus of Saxony, with the arms of Lithuania and Poland, the die without doubt was picked up during Friederich's conquest of Saxony. This is called the Augustdor (See

Gumowski 2195). Bruno Kisch, "Judaica in Nummis," also refers to "the rare Prussian Hoym thaler, the Hoym Friedrichsdor, etc. issued by Hirsch Simon and Isaac Daniel Itzig in Breslau on August 20, 1781" — the reference being to Count Karl von Hoym, the top minister in the Silesian government and a friend of the Jews. These quasi-personal strikes have been given names like Ephraimiten, etc.

93. Quoted in Selma Stern, **The Court Jew**, p. 176.

94. **Encyclopaedia Judaica** (Berlin: Verlag Eschkol A. -G., 1928), p. 950. Also Samuel Poznanski, "Babylonische Geonim im nach-gaonäischen Zeitalter nach handschriftlichen und gedruckten Quellen," **Schriften der Lehranstalt für die Wissenschaft des Judentums**, Band IV (Berlin: Mayer und Muller, 1914), p. 133.

95. Information about Yemen obtained from the late Dr. Cecil Roth. It is also certain that Jews were mint masters in North African states like Morocco, but there is almost no source material.

96. Other Jewish mint employees flourished in Europe after this date, but their main renown was in the field of medals, and they will be discussed under that category. Excluded from this study are Jewish mint masters in the state of Israel. Mention, however, should be made of Samuel Kretschmer, who organized a mint in Jerusalem under the name of S. Kretschmer & Sons. Though many of Israel's coins and medals have been struck in Berne, Switzerland, San Francisco, U.S.A., and Utrecht, the Netherlands, the Kretschmer Mint also issued coins and medals.

97. It should not be forgotten that we for the most part know of these Jewish mint masters and Court Jews only by accident from Christian sources. There must have been many other such persons, now unknown, especially in the small courts of Central Europe. For example, the writer has encountered a reference to "Jean le Juif, trésorier royal à Toulouse" (John, the Jew, royal treasurer at Toulouse); see **Cahiers de la Commission française des Archives juives**, No. 4 (Paris, 1965—1966), p. 5. As another example, one source (without quoting documentation) states that Levko — an important banker and mint master for Casimir the Great of Poland — was his court treasurer as well. Much work still remains to be done on this subject.

98. Jews in other areas of the Moslem world were likewise in positions of authority. Yakub ben Killis, a banker, converted to Islam and was appointed Egyptian minister of finance in 976 and vizier in 977. Almost three centuries later Sad ad-Doula, a physician, became grand vizier of Iraq. Appointing one of his brothers governor of Baghdad and another governor of Mosul, he aroused enmity and was murdered by a court conspiracy in 1291.

Chapter II. Jewish Medalists

1. **Encyclopaedia Judaica, s.v.** "Seals" (Jerusalem: Keter Publishing House Ltd., 1971), Vol. 14, p. 1079.

2. The traditional use of the Hebrew "ben" for son, in this case ben Abram, now became fixed in the last name as Abram's son or Abramson.

3. Christian IV was a witty man. When a German pastor dedicated an anti-Semitic pamphlet to him, the Danish king wrote back that he had just appointed a second Jew, Benjamin Musaphia, to assist his personal physician, Daniel de Castro.

4. L. Forrer's **Biographical Dictionary of Medallists** (London: Spink & Son Ltd.) is a veritable bible for information about medalists. Inevitably, given the eight volumes, errors creep in. Forrer lists an Alfred Jacobson as well but, according to authoritative sources, "Alfred" is the same person as Albert Jacobson.

5. **The Coin Cabinet**, Issue No. 5 of the Historical Museum of Frankfurt on Main (1964), item 41.

6. Franz Landsberger, **A History of Jewish Art** (Cincinnati, Ohio: The Union of American Hebrew Congregations, 1964), p. 230. No source material is quoted, though Cecil Roth repeats this reference several times in later publications.

7. Material extracted from E. Stchukin, **Medallic Art in Russia of the XVIIIth Century** (Leningrad, 1962), p. 118; and Julius Iversen, **Dictionary of Medallists and Other Persons Whose Names Appear on Russian Medals** (St. Petersburg, 1874), p. 5.

8. Ernest Babelon in his **La Gravure en Pierres fines** (Paris, 1894) states that Jean-Henri Simon was a great-grandson of Thomas Simon, the excellent 17th-century English medalist. This seems impossible, for there is irrefutable proof that Thomas Simon was a Protestant. As for Jean-Henri Simon himself, there is no question of his religion, for the grand rabbi of Belgium gave the funeral sermon when he was buried with military honors at Brussels.

9. There was mutual affection among the brothers, and they often collaborated with one another.

10. A cryptic reference is made in the 1907 **Jewish Encyclopedia**, s.v. "Engravers," Vol. V, p. 177, to a man named Saphir, "a clever stone engraver" who "has done some work for the court of Russia." Nothing is known beyond this single sentence, but it is a fact that a few Jews were exempt from the anti-Semitic court ban. Albert Wolf also refers to a Saphir who lived in Karlsbad; see his **Etwas über jüdische Kunst und ältere jüdische Künstler** (Hamburg, 1902), p. 21. It is not clear whether the two references indicate the same person, though Wolf also states that Saphir's work was in the possession of the Russian Court.

11. Considering that the Griliches lived in just the last century, there is remarkable confusion surrounding their lives. No two

reference books seem to agree on dates or activities. The writer has followed what seems more authoritative opinion throughout, especially the Griliches articles in the **Yevreiskaya Entziklopedija** (St. Petersburg, 1908–1913), Vol. 6, col. 783–784.

12. The literature on René Stern never makes unequivocally clear whether he was the engraver or only the editor of die cutting for these medals.

13. Excluded from this list is Karl Lesser, 1783–1849, who was the last official to hold the post of Medalist to the Mint at Breslau. Lesser was a top Prussian medalist and did medals of the nobility. Among his pieces is the 1837 portrait of the distinguished Dr. Elias Henschel, a Jew from Breslau. Considering the name plus the place of origin, and the fact that Lesser was a pupil of Abramson, there is great justification for considering him of Jewish origin. But we have no source material alluding to that matter, though Dr. Moritz Stern in **Aus dem Berliner Jüdischen Museum** (Berlin, 1937), did list him as a Jewish medalist.

14. There have been reports that the very famous Austrian mint master and medalist, Professor Stefan Schwartz, was a baptized Jew. But the evidence is too insubstantial to warrant his inclusion. In fact, the impression received on reading **Medaillen und Plaketten in Ungarn** (p. 360), by Procopius and Huszar, is the reverse. The writer is familiar with two portrait medals of Jewish interest struck by Schwartz: that of Anton Bettelheim, the Austrian critic and journalist, and the 1911 portrait of Dr. Alfred Stern.

15. First reference in Albert Wolf, **Etwas über jüdische Kunst (Nachtrag)**; second in L. Forrer, **Biographical Dictionary of Medallists.**

16. Excluded is Josef V. Myslbek (1848–1922), the top sculptor of 19th-century Bohemia and an excellent medalist as well. Though Catholic, his father (Misbeck) was Jewish. His three best-known medals are: the Prague Chamber of Commerce, from 1888; Jindrich (Henry) Fuegner, dated 1903; and Miroslav Tyrs, dated 1904. The two portrait medals honored the cofounders of the Sokol movement.

17. Jewish medalists from Poland are almost unknown. It might be mentioned, however, that at the 13th Congress of the International Federation of the Medal, held in 1969 at Prague, among the Polish entries was a Bernard Lewinski. Only a dozen Polish medals were illustrated in the Catalogue, but among these was Mr. Lewinski's "Birds." By the name, Bernard Lewinski is Jewish or of Jewish origin.

18. Mention might also be made of the late-18th-century David Alves Rebello, an English Jew of Renaissance proclivities. Rebello in 1795 commissioned the "Hackney Promissory Token," which has the honor of being considered the first private token ever issued in England. Rebello, of course, was not the medalist.

19. Actually, Myer Myers, the very famous 18th-century New York silversmith, did several circumcision medals. We have descriptions, but none can now be located.

20. Furst medals, including all those mentioned, can be purchased at very reasonable prices from the Superintendent, United States Mint, Philadelphia, Pa. 19130. They are restruck in light bronze.

21. Certain Jewish medalists are excluded from this analysis because the writer has been unable to discover more detailed information. They include A. Tennenbaum, who did a medal of Baron Maurice de Hirsch; a certain Schapiry, who engraved Samuel Horowitz at Lvov, Poland, in 1911; B. Simon, with his 1953 portrait piece of the architect Erich Mendelsohn; Margit Newman, who did Sholom Asch and Julius H. Kahn, both in 1941; and Elisabeth Seligmann, from Hamburg. In the early 20th century Palestine, Moses Murro and Max Farbmann also did interesting folk medals.

22. Brenner also engraved four coins in 1897 for the Dominican Republic.

23. The social and political atmosphere of 19th- and 20th-century Hungary resembled that of 19th-century Germany, in which Jews were barred from many professions unless they became Christians. This created many nominal baptisms similar to that of the self-mocking Heinrich Heine.

24. Zadkine, who was born in 1890 at Smolensk, Russia, and died in 1967 at Paris, also did a few medals. The writer has seen only a stylized joint portrait of Theo and Vincent van Gogh, executed in 1964.

25. Alfred Rothberger, the early 20th-century Viennese sculptor and medalist, has not been included, for the writer can find no information on his background. His best-known medals are portraits of Frederic Chopin, Th. Leschitizky, A. Door, Berthe Marx-Goldschmidt, and Gustav Mahler, the last two being of interest to the Jewish collector.

26. The most complete listing of Hungarian medalists and their production can be found in **Medaillen-und Plaketten-kunst in Ungarn,** by Procopius and Huszár.

27. In recent years la Monnaie has broadened its policy, and le Club français de la Médaille has gone far beyond a parochial policy, embracing all human culture.

28. Leon Zack, born in 1892 in Russia and a long-time Parisian, is a converted Jew. Under the influence of the famed Theilhard de Chardin, he has become a fervent Catholic and works extensively as a Church decorator. In 1966 Zack did a portrait medal of Father Sertillanges. In more recent years he has done three rather abstract medals, Impression, Floral, and Homage to Cubism.

29. The recent revelation that Lenin's mother was born a Jew-

ess, not contested by Soviet authorities, adds more interest to this particular medal for the Jewish collector.

30. Mico Kaufman, now a resident of Massachusetts but a former inmate of a concentration camp, did the obverse side of the official presidential inaugural medal of Gerald R. Ford. Kaufman also did the official Ford vice-presidential inaugural medal.

31. A few similar plaques were also done by Lotte Philip, German by origin, who became a Professor of Art at Queens College.

32. The late Ben Shahn (1898–1969), who was born in Russia but became an American citizen at the age of eight, designed in the last year of his life the 20 Years Anniversary medal for El Al, the Israeli national airline.

Index

Italicized page number indicates illustration